3

741.6092 MYE

DESIGN: THE WORLD OF

Minale Tattersfield

EDITED BY EDWARD BOOTH · CLIBBORN
WRITTEN BY JEREMY MYERSON

Editor	**Edward Booth-Clibborn**
Written by	**Jeremy Myerson**
Book Design	**Minale Tattersfield & Partners**
Art Direction	**Marcello Minale, Ian Glazer**
Designers	**Lucy Northway, Ian Glazer, Sarah Praill**
Illustration	**Brian Tattersfield**
Typeset by	**Acesetters Limited**
Printed by	**Toppan Printing Company**

Published in Europe by: Internos Books, 18 Colville Road, London W3 8BL, England. World Direct Rights: Internos Books ISBN No. 0904866777. America and Canada, Trade Books, Letraset USA, 40 Eisenhower Drive, Paramus, NJ 07652, USA.
Direct Mail, American Illustration Books, 49 East 21st Street, New York, NY 10010, USA. Rest of the World Distribution: Hearst Books International, 105 Madison Avenue, New York, NY 10016, USA.

contents

38 travel & **leisure**

96 commercial & **industrial**

124 publishing & **media**

164 banking & **finance**

188 food & **drink**

224 shopping & **fashion**

Edward Booth-Clibborn

This book is much more than a simple record. It is a celebration: a joyous exposition of the use of art to communicate ideas with wit, simplicity and intelligence. **For** over twenty five years now, this has been Minale Tattersfield's forte. Since the beginning, their objective has been the same: to define their clients' problems

foreword

precisely and to solve them with startling clarity. **Their** insight into other people's businesses has fed their own business management so that today, Minale Tattersfield is an international concern with offices all round the world. Yet the same principle still informs every project undertaken. **First** comes the idea. Then comes the execution. That's how they approach design. **Welcome** then, to the world of Minale Tattersfield.

Edward Booth-Clibborn
Chairman, D&AD London

Jeremy Myerson is a leading
commentator on international
design. He founded the world's
first weekly design magazine,
DesignWeek, and is also a former
editor of Creative Review. He has
worked as a senior editor on
Design and has been published in
The Guardian, The Observer,
The Times and The Financial Times.

As a journalist and commentator covering the international design scene, I first became aware of the enormous impact and individuality of Minale Tattersfield & Partners in 1982, when the consultancy staged a show of its work at the London Design Centre. **The** attraction was immediate: here were designers whose approach was simple yet

preface

sophisticated. They were capable of solving horrendously complicated commercial problems with an ease and wit which summed up for me how good design should always be: so unforced and elegant that it appears obvious. **Interestingly** enough, that 1982 exhibition in London proved to be the springboard for Minale Tattersfield's international advance during the 1980s, an advance which now ranks the group in the world top ten in terms of size and, I suspect, a good deal higher in terms of creative calibre. **In** 1986 Edward Booth-Clibborn published a book about the consultancy, Design à la Minale Tattersfield, which explored its artist-designer origins in the creative ferment of the early 1960s and charted its spectacular tradition of invention up to the mid-80s. That book was a sell-out. **This** new volume takes up the story at a time of transition. How could Minale Tattersfield apply its special brand of logic and magic to the increasing 'globalisation' of design? How could it tailor solutions to multinational as well as local clients?

The World of Minale Tattersfield charts the group's progress and achievements in a variety of international markets. It maps out 25 years of design innovation and takes us right into the 1990s, with the lasting quality of the work the common denominator despite a wide spectrum of different cultures and contexts – from Italian fashion and Spanish retailing to Japanese chemicals and consumer goods. **The** link in this book between the newer work shown and some of the earlier timeless designs first seen in Design à la Minale Tattersfield reveals the continuity and consistency of a deceptively simple approach. The problems are getting harder but the solutions have the same measured creative authority. **The** work in this volume is divided into six categories – Travel & Leisure, Commercial & Industrial, Publishing & Media, Banking & Finance, Food & Drink, and Shopping & Fashion – which highlight the sectors so important in providing design commissions in recent years. **These** are preceded by two essays which take a look first at the phenomenal growth of the international design market in the 1980s, and then at the artistic and cultural influences which have helped to shape Minale Tattersfield's unique response to it.

Jeremy Myerson

Jeremy Myerson

London   Osaka

Paris   New York

Cologne   Casablanca

Barcelona   Hong Kong

Madrid   Brisbane

Milan   Sydney

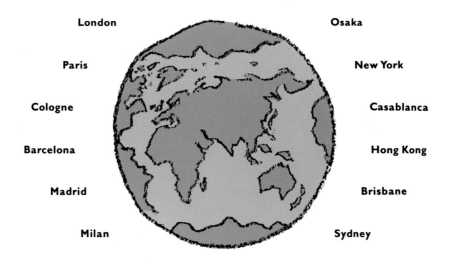

Minale Tattersfield Design Strategy

The partners and associates of
Minale Tattersfield Design Strategy at
their first international conference
15th November 1989.

1 Leon Angel (UK).	**8** Ian Glazer (UK).	**15** Frances Magee (UK).	**22** David Hawkins (France).
2 David Liu (Hong Kong).	**9** Hiroshi Onishi (Hong Kong).	**16** Ian Delaney (UK).	**23** Susan Smith (UK).
3 Michael Bryce (Australia).	**10** Brian Tattersfield (UK).	**17** Toti Melzi D'Eril (Italy).	**24** Mary Cunniff (USA).
4 Liza Hurtley (UK).	**11** Claude Meillet (France).	**18** Philippe Rasquinet (France).	**25** Neville Blech (UK).
5 Francisco Garcia Ruescas (Spain).	**12** Nigel MacFall (UK).	**19** Sandro Cabrini (Italy).	**26** Nobuoki Ohtani (UK).
6 Ian Grindle (UK).	**13** Marcello Minale (UK).	**20** Ida Morazzoni (Italy).	**27** Marian Hawkins (UK).
7 Jim Waters (France).	**14** Dimitri Karavias (UK).	**21** Alex Maranzano (UK).	**28** Jean-Louis Duclos (France).

There is no rational reason why periods of social and economic change should come parcelled up in neat ten-year packages. Nevertheless design historians appear to have an irresistible urge to draw a line at the start of each new decade and apply labels of convenience to the preceding era – the Festival of Britain Fifties or the Pop Art Sixties,

advances

for example. **Often**, they are thwarted in describing such simplistic boundaries of change. Pop, Punk and Post-Modernism all emerged to make a significant impression when the decades to which they belonged – the '60s, '70s and '80s respectively – were well under-way. Unpredictable cultural movements have no respect for artificial compartments. But the obsession with the all-purpose unit of the decade remains – to mark our advances in society, and the way these are reflected in the design of artefacts, environments and communications all around us. **We** now stand on the threshold of the 1990s – a new decade with a new set of expectations in design. But as in the natural way of these things, many of the developments which will become evident in this decade have been in rehearsal during the preceding one. The 1980s proved to be a time of radical change in design – not just in its outward manifestation via an eclecticism of style, but in the way it was practised by professional designers. **For** the first time there was a consistent and concentrated application of business management techniques in the way design consultants – once known simply as commercial artists – went about their business. The result was that a creative process with the individual artist-designer at its centre was transformed into a team effort with many different disciplines – marketing, design, accounting – sharing roles. **Design** projects became larger and more complicated in the 1980s just as design groups became larger and more complicated. Multinational client companies exploring new opportunities in world trade sought out multi-disciplinary design consultants to service their international needs. **British** design in particular took on an international dimension, with UK design firms investing in design markets in Europe, North America and the Pacific Basin. Designers started the 1980s as stylists; by its close they had become strategists. Many had even floated their companies on the Stock Market, or expanded their workforce beyond the size of the clients who commissioned them. **Did** all this activity happen conveniently within the ten-year span known as the 1980s? The groundwork was surely laid in the late '70s but there are some crucial pointers to observe at the start of the decade.

1960's

If you look back, you can see the first move by Allied International Designers (a company now absorbed into another) to achieve City credibility with a Stock Exchange listing in 1980; a Downing Street design summit in 1982 at which Mrs Thatcher laid the path for sustained government seedcorn investment in funding design consultancy; and the first flowering of a 'revolution' in retail design with the opening of the Next chain in 1982, which brought the skills of designers to the forefront of economic change. **What** emerged were the characteristics of a multi-million-pound industry. Many design companies started to behave like big businesses, recruiting marketing and sales staff, acquiring subsidiary firms and opening new offices around the world in a bid to establish what are fashionably known as 'global design networks.' Some design groups joined larger advertising, marketing and communications-based conglomerates to gain instant access to a network, to share resources and information, and to enjoy client cross-referrals. **International** work was clearly essential to the future of British design, given the parlous state of UK manufacturing, but it was no longer simply a question of getting on a plane. The rules of the game had changed: expensive strategies were in play, new connections were being made and unforeseen alliances forged.

For those design consultancies with an established track record of work for international clients,

1947·1967

such as Minale Tattersfield & Partners, the 1980s – the design era when market capitalisation took over from the magic marker – called for a reassessment. **Of** course, overseas commissions were nothing new. Neither for that matter were global design networks. When a pioneering group of American designers, Raymond Loewy, Henry Dreyfuss and Norman Bel Geddes among them, effectively founded the modern international design consulting business in America in the years directly after the 1929 Wall Street Crash, they targeted multinational clients. By 1946 Loewy in particular could claim to be designing for most major world markets. **Later** in the 1960s, the world's first truly global design operation was established, entitled Unimark International. Originating from Chicago and featuring such well-established designers as Massimo Vignelli, Ralph Eckerstrom and Bob Norda, Unimark opened a string of offices throughout America, Europe and the Far East. At its peak it employed 500 staff but it was a concept ahead of its time. The economic recession of the early '70s, in particular the oil crisis and three-day-week in Britain, brought it to its knees. Industrial unrest at its major client, Ford, dealt the final blow. **The** 1980s, though, presented a different story. At last designers were organising and managing their affairs in a way which enabled them to build larger companies capable of withstanding the pressure of international markets. Achieving this commercial

1970's

and managerial robustness, however, often entailed considerable sacrifice in terms of creative quality. **As** the decade wore on, so the dilemma increased. How could designers expand their activities in international markets and yet retain the creative vision and flexibility so vital to producing effective and exciting design solutions? How could consultants make the bridge from the old world of commercial artistry to the new world of multinational strategy without abandoning the very principles which characterised their profession? **Nobody** with any ambition in British design was immune from this soul-searching. Commentators and analysts were particularly intrigued by the position of Minale Tattersfield, which enjoyed a reputation as a world leader in design and had an impressive roster of international clients. How could Minale Tattersfield consolidate and enhance its standing in the world design market at a time of rapid change and escalating competition without falling into the trap of making creative compromises? **This** was indeed a challenge. Minale Tattersfield is a name associated with wit and ideas in design, with the swiftness of thought and freedom of expression associated with a small, highly mobile company. How could the consultancy's partners find a route to keep this special talent intact? **The** formula for growth chosen by Minale Tattersfield has been characteristically tailored to suit its own philosophy and ideals. Nobody else could have done it in quite the same way.

ITALIAN KNITWEAR EXHIBITION
Italian Trade Centre, 20 Savile Row, London W1
14-17 October 1975. 10am-6pm

That is because the consultancy, which was founded in 1964 by Marcello Minale and Brian Tattersfield, has always followed its own individualistic and idiosyncratic path, remaining aloof from the mainstream and unbending in its commitment to quality. **It** has been a sophisticated softly-softly approach. The British magazine DesignWeek described Minale Tattersfield as 'the dark horse stealing up in international markets'. The dark horse is now one of the leaders in the field; it is among the top ten design groups in the world according to the Financial Times. But as Marcello Minale says, 'our ambition is to be the best, not the biggest. Expansion around the world has been because of one reason – demand from clients.' **A** more detailed look at the nature of Minale Tattersfield's international progress tells us much about design in the 1980s – and provides some clues about what to expect this decade. A landmark for the consultancy came in 1981 when Minale Tattersfield was invited to stage an exhibition of its work at the London Design Centre. The show, featuring designs developed over an 18-year period, was widely acclaimed by press and public. **Within** four years, Minale Tattersfield was being invited overseas by various public authorities to hold exhibitions of its work in European and Far Eastern cities, so that designers and clients here could analyse its approach. **The** first was in 1983 at the Padiglione D'Arte Contemporanea in Milan, a showpiece institution for top European design.

1980's

The design elite of Milan turned out in force for the opening and leading Italian newspaper
La Repubblica wrote up the show under the banner headline: 'Vent'Anni di magia grafica, approdano
in Via Palestro.' (Twenty years of graphic magic has landed in Via Palestro). Minale Tattersfield's work
was dubbed 'communication with a smile' by Mercedes Garberi, director of Milan's civic collections.
This was followed by an invitation to exhibit at the Centro Cultural de la Villa de Madrid. The show
coincided with Spain's entry into the common market and was opened by the British ambassador.
Then, in 1988, Minale Tattersfield looked east with a Japanese exhibition at the Axis Gallery in Tokyo
– just as it had looked west with work selected for the permanent design collection of the Museum of
Modern Art in New York. What the consultancy was doing in entering the select world of exhibitions
and museums was effectively bridging the gulf between art and commerce. **The** Milan, Madrid and
Tokyo shows also had a tangible effect on the consultancy's business: they attracted large crowds
(50,000 saw both the Spanish and Italian exhibitions and 40,000 went to the Axis Gallery) and this in
turn stimulated demand for Minale Tattersfield design. A nucleus of clients began to emerge in each of
these markets. To deal with the demand, Minale Tattersfield appointed marketing agents to service
companies in a particular country, with all the main design work being carried out in the group's

Bull worldwide
information systems

London studios. So the first three overseas marketing offices opened in Milan, Madrid and Cologne. **The** formula was then repeated in Hong Kong, Osaka and New York. But Australia, an emerging design market in the Pacific which Marcello Minale had inspected on close quarters during an extensive lecture tour, posed a different problem. Many of the group's Japanese clients were operating in the Australian market so an extension of its design activities from its Tokyo bridgehead appeared logical. But the sheer distance and time differences called for a new approach. **The** solution was found in a tie-up with Brisbane and Sydney graphic design firm Bryce Design to form Minale Tattersfield Bryce in autumn 1988. Michael Bryce's belief in the subtle intellect at the heart of all good design made him a natural candidate to be a partner and ally of Minale Tattersfield. He has an architectural background which he draws on to create graphics for leisure and tourism, and his prestigious client list includes the National Trust of Australia, the International Culture Corporation of Australia and the City of Brisbane. **Closer** to home, Minale Tattersfield then turned its attention to the French market, which is vital to success in Europe. France is fiercely nationalistic and has always been regarded by designers as difficult to negotiate with successfully. However, Minale Tattersfield enjoyed a reputation in France as a European rather than British design firm and the group had also built a presence there with work

Australian
National Trust

for BP and Lever. Even so, it opted again to expand the partnership on which the consultancy has always been based. **A** merger with Paris-based Design Strategy in autumn 1989 created a new Anglo-French axis in design, and brought five new partners into the fold – Belgian Philippe Rasquinet, American Jim Waters, Frenchmen Jean-Louis Duclos and Claude Meillet, and Englishman David Hawkins. It also added such leading clients as Rhône-Poulenc, Bull and Banque Nationale de Paris (BNP) to the client list. **Now** Minale Tattersfield Design Strategy has more than 130 designers, and three design studios in London, Paris and Brisbane, supported by nine marketing offices in Madrid, Milan, Brussels, Cologne, Casablanca, Hong Kong, Sydney, Osaka and New York. The consultancy is not a colossus. That was never the intention. But it has the presence, knowhow and resources worldwide to carry out major international projects for multinational clients. In a design field full of advertising-based communications conglomerates, the group offers a clear alternative. **Minale Tattersfield's** international advance is significant in a number of ways. By achieving a broader strategic reach without losing its roots in the artist-designer tradition, the group has managed to produce work which lives up to Marcello Minale's dictum that 'creative integrity must be maintained with growth'. But the evolving nature of the organisation also says much about design in the 1990s. After the blanket

Union de Banques
à Paris

business globalism of design and style in the 1980s, observers now suggest that the way forward is towards more regional and local flavour in design, and more use of art and craft to differentiate products and services. That is because a consensus of approach to international marketing in business circles and a plateau of creative proficiency in design circles has led to much homogeneity and blandness in the design of environments, products and communications. **The** new tenor of the age is summed up in the doctrine, 'Think globally, act locally.' This means that while an international perspective is essential, design solutions must be developed with sensitivity to local markets and not simply be imposed through worldwide economies of scale in planning and production. In a sense, Minale Tattersfield is well-placed to benefit from these changes in market and management theory because its entire international direction has been tied to specific locality, to art and originality, rather than the imposition of an anonymous brand of global design. **But** of course Minale Tattersfield has no monopoly on wisdom and no reliable crystal ball. If the 1980s taught us one thing, it was to expect the unexpected. As Brian Tattersfield remarks: 'Design practice in the '90s will change all the time because the problems we are asked to solve will change all the time.' Already the map of world design is being dramatically redrawn as Eastern Europe opens its doors to more liberated economic

ways and the Pacific Rim begins to realise its potential. And new technological developments – from high-speed computer plotting to super-tough composite materials – are set to change the designer's impact on the material world. **Marcello Minale** is mindful of the way Europe's leading fashion houses such as Valentino and Armani (both, incidentally, Minale Tattersfield clients) have sold the European idea of style and dressing throughout the world. He believes it is possible to do the same with design. 'In America and Japan, design is more formal and technical,' he explains. 'But European design is less regimented and still allows lateral thinking. That's a tremendous opportunity.' **It** could well be that design appeals more to the irrational and emotional side of consumers than the rational in the 1990s, demanding problem-solving of a more lateral nature. But amid much uncertainty about the future, one thing is clear. Minale Tattersfield will be in the vanguard of change in international design during the 1990s, just as it forged ahead during the 1980s. That is the group's natural position.

1990's

The famous scribble – a timeless symbol
proclaiming that scribbled ideas are more
valid than the polite moving about of
shapes and type.

The idea of a group of designers and artists of complementary skills working together is not a twentieth century phenomenon. In 18th century England, the Classicist interior designer Robert Adam employed as many as 2,000 craftsmen, cabinetmakers, sculptors and decorative painters at the peak of his business career. Many of Adam's harmonious interiors

influences

survive to this day at places like Syon Park and Osterley Park in London; one has even been lovingly taken intact from a now demolished country house to be integrated in the new high-tech Lloyds Building. They serve as proof of an earlier age of organisation and shared experience in creating design. **But** what has distinguished the practice of design this century has been the conscious balance struck between artistic perception and technical skill in assembling design teams. Each designer brings to the group a background, training and attitude shaped by a diverse range of social, cultural and artistic influences. How those influences are expressed within a group dynamic determines the nature and content of the design created. **At** the Bauhaus in

Germany in the 1920s there was a self-conscious experiment in cross-fertilising branches of the visual arts. Bauhaus director Walter Gropius encouraged the interplay of design, craft, sculpture, fine art and modelmaking in order to discover new forms and meanings in design. A decade later, in the more commercial environment of the 'New Deal' America, the pioneering group of US consultants who shaped the international design consulting business – men such as Raymond Loewy, Norman Bel Geddes, Henry Dreyfuss and Walter Dorwin Teague – drew on diverse backgrounds and skills in the absence of any existing industrial design role model in commerce. **These** men had trained in many adjacent fields – from stage design and fashion illustration to photography and display. In the aftermath of the Wall Street Crash they drew these diverse strands together to create an approach to industrial design which enabled hard-pressed US industry to gain new markets with more attractive consumer products. **What** has been at work in design ever since shopping centres replaced churches as cathedrals of the people, since Classicism gave way to Modernism, and since the machine usurped the hand and eye in production, has been a measuring of rational organisation and planning against the intuitive nature of artistic influence. **Study** of these influences is instrumental to understanding the philosophy and outlook of any group of designers – and this is particularly so in the case of

Minale Tattersfield which offers a particularly rich and diverse set of influences via the backgrounds and temperaments of its six UK-based partners. **It** has been said that the key to the consultancy's approach is that it makes style the servant of the solution. Its work has also been described as simple, detached and cool yet at the same time witty, warm and humorous. These two conflicting strands, which are repeatedly reconciled in the consultancy's work, can be found in the backgrounds of the founding partners, Marcello Minale and Brian Tattersfield. **Marcello Minale** grew up in post-war Naples, at a time of reconstruction in Italian society. He initially studied architecture at technical college, but he was greatly influenced by the work of the leading Finnish designer Tapio Wirkkala, who was closely associated with the Scandinavian Modern Movement. **Wirkkala** had, in the words of Minale, 'reinvented the straight line'. His work in furniture, lamps and particularly glassware introduced Minale to a new design style a world away from the baroque Neapolitan household in which he had grown up. Wirkkala's glassware designs for the Finnish company Iittala, which also commissioned the great Alvar Aalto, brought him international acclaim. In particular he emerged on to the world stage via the Milan Triennale in the early 1950s. His clients included such legendary manufacturers as Rosenthal and Venini, and he went on to collaborate with the charismatic Raymond Loewy.

Glassware
by Tapio Wirkkala

Duly inspired by Tapio Wirkkala, Minale went to Finland for a year to study industrial design and that influence has remained with him ever since. However, a counterbalancing influence to Finnish cool also made itself felt early in Minale's career. The humour of French illustrators Savignac and André François impressed on Minale the need to put the idea first in graphics. The irrepressible mixture of the simple, detached view and the witty idea is evident throughout Minale Tattersfield's portfolio.

Brian Tattersfield enjoyed early artistic influences rather closer to home than Finland to Naples. He grew up in the West Riding of Yorkshire in an environment in which he was encouraged to paint and draw. His father designed window displays for a local rètailing chain and his elder brother Gordon was a painter who studied at the Royal College of Art (Brian subsequently followed him). Gordon's influences at the RCA – Francis Bacon, Keith Vaughan and Graham Sutherland – also became influences on Brian. In particular their control of the canvas, and mastery of colour and ideas, had a compelling effect. **Together** the two Tattersfield brothers would indulge a passion for architecture; they built countless models and had a huge collection of plans of buildings. When Brian Tattersfield went to art school, it was with every intention of becoming a painter. 'But', he says, 'I was far more interested in the story-telling content so I was obviously an illustrator, not a painter.' **As** an art student in the

Illustrations

by André François

1950s, Tattersfield encountered the work of New York painters and graphic artists Ben Shahn and Saul Steinberg. Just as Steinberg painted streetscapes onto furniture, so Tattersfield turned his grandmother's kitchen table into a hotel. (Tattersfield's interest in architecture in art has been enduring, culminating in 1987 with the design of a set of stamps of British Architects for the Royal Mail.) **Between** Batley Art College and the RCA, Tattersfield spent two years doing National Service in the RAF. He must have been the only regular airman subscribing at that time to Vogue: it says much for his character that he could follow visual style amid the gloom of austerity Britain. Tattersfield also visited the London Design Centre and discovered that there were people who actually designed knives and forks, machines and spades. Commercial art for production? The idea was irresistible in its simplicity. **Brian Tattersfield's** time at the RCA as a contemporary of David Hockney at the dawning of the Sixties introduced him to more cultural influences. 'It was an exciting period,' he recalls. 'The early Sixties set out to demolish the Fifties and there wasn't the barrier then between fine art and design there is now.' **The** guest lectures and design work of two Americans – Charles Eames in furniture and Saul Bass in film titles (Tattersfield ran the RCA film society) had a particular effect. St Louis-born Eames had been the first designer of any nationality

Chair
by Charles Eames with
Saul Steinberg drawing

to stage a one-man show at New York's Museum of Modern Art in 1947. His bent plywood and steel furniture for Herman Miller in the 1950s contributed to his reputation as America's most influential industrial design spokesman; and he went on to combine interests in interior design with activities in experimental film. A short film entitled Powers of Ten he had made in 1949, about a house in Santa Monica he built entirely from mass-produced components, became a cult movie. **New York**-born Saul Bass, meanwhile, turned the film title sequence from a banal list of credits into a special section contributing to the atmosphere of the film, with a life and integrity all of its own. His work on Alfred Hitchcock's Psycho and Otto Preminger's The Man With The Golden Arm added fresh dimension to cinema titles, and Bass went on to establish his name in corporate America with identity programmes for AT&T, Warner Communications and United Airlines. **What** Charles Eames and Saul Bass taught Tattersfield was that you could develop a view of problem-solving in design which extended across a wide range of disciplines and commercial contexts. **Brian Tattersfield** was also influenced by the work of André François (the French illustrator is an enthusiasm shared with Minale), but he believes that the American designer Bob Gill, who came over to London from New York, did most to 'make the link between the visual world of the painting student and how to use it to

New Yorker cover
by André François

communicate something'. At the RCA, Gill introduced Tattersfield to the marvellous world of the New Yorker, to the art direction of Esquire, and to the Volkswagen campaigns of Doyle Dane Bernbach which were changing the face of advertising. **Other** designers, notably the typographer Herb Lubalin, are credited by Tattersfield with helping to shape his direction. Lubalin was a New York typographer and art director whose distinctive personal style was highly visible on posters, packs, magazines and advertisements: he often impacted letterforms against each other to create arresting images out of type, or played visual tricks to create double-entendres in graphics. **By** the time Brian Tattersfield left the RCA, the essence of the Minale Tattersfield philosophy was in place: to use art to communicate the idea with wit, simplicity and intelligence. **The** consultancy's four other UK-based partners are also RCA graduates; in a sense, the ethos of Kensington Gore is all-pervasive. Two of the partners, Alex Maranzano and Ian Grindle, joined Minale Tattersfield directly from college, so the work of the two founders has naturally been an important influence. Maranzano, who joined the consultancy in 1968, talks of his excitement at seeing Minale Tattersfield's design for Alitalia's twentieth birthday – a runway of candles on a cake – for the first time. 'Brian and Marcello made everyone else look so dull', he remarks. **There** are also strands of continuity in other cultural influences: Ian Grindle,

Cover
by Bob Gill
Volkswagen ad
by Doyle Dane
Bernbach

whose first degree was at Ravensbourne, admits to being influenced by David Hockney and Bob Gill, both of whom were active in Brian Tattersfield's time at the RCA. Grindle also credits RCA head of department Lou Klein, who once worked with Michael Peters, as influential in promoting the New York school of graphics in which creativity and good ideas count for everything. **Ian Grindle's** first conscious awareness of an interest in design manifested itself in collecting concert tickets and studying the typography. He is still a great collector of everyday ephemera, a magpie of the material world. His random collections feed many valuable ideas into the consultancy, says Brian Tattersfield.

Alex Maranzano, meanwhile, can draw on the artistic sources of a cosmopolitan background. He was born in France of Italian parents and came to Britain at the age of five. At art school he became steeped in Italian Renaissance art, although he admits his greatest love is for the French painters – Degas, Cézanne, Gauguin and Lautrec. 'The sheer drive that oozed out of those individuals makes everything seem possible,' he says. **As** a lettering designer at Camberwell art school in the early Sixties, Maranzano was naturally influenced by Eric Gill and Edward Johnson. Gill in particular was a vivid figure for the lettering student: a prolific engraver, sculptor, writer and type designer who created the Gill Sans typeface for the Monotype Corporation. Gill possessed a romantic and mystical approach to the handicrafts, but his belief in an 'all-pervading truth in the making of simple objects' significantly shaped Maranzano's thinking. **Later**, at the RCA, the 'concept' started to creep into Alex Maranzano's design language as the work of Robert Brownjohn, Saul Bass and Bob Gill had an effect – just as it had on the work of his mentors. **For** a number of years, Minale Tattersfield had just four partners. Then, in April 1988, a new partner joined. Not surprisingly, he is an RCA graduate – but in every other way Nobuoki Ohtani is cut from very different cloth. **Oki**, as he is known, is a Japanese industrial designer with extensive international experience who has brought a new dimension – and a fresh set of cultural influences – to Minale Tattersfield. Like Brian Tattersfield, Oki was much influenced by his elder brother, who became an industrial designer, and by his father, who was an oil painter. He grew up in Tokyo and for a long time weighed up the choice between becoming a fine artist or a designer. He studied silversmithing and sculpture – but also teamed up with his brother to design ski equipment. **Oki's** first car was a Fiat 500 and in the early Seventies he left Japan and went to Italy to learn about European design, an early influence on his work. He holds the designs of Italian maestro Mario Bellini in high esteem today. Bellini is one of the great contemporary names in Milanese design, a consultant to such leading companies as Cassina, Artemide,

Engraving
by Eric Gill
Gill Sans typeface
by Eric Gill

Flos, Fiat and Olivetti. It was with Olivetti in particular that Bellini established his reputation: machines were given a metaphorical quality which transcended their everyday function; typewriters and word processors took on a sculptural presence. **The** ability of the Italians to invest objects with meaning has never been lost on Oki. He came to London in 1973 and decided to study under industrial design professor Misha Black at the RCA. Black had co-founded Britain's first design consultancy, Design Research Unit, in 1944 with Milner Gray, a venture which drew inspiration from the example of Loewy and his peers in America in the 1930s. Black was one of the outstanding design educationalists of the post-war era, doing much to break down barriers between engineers and designers in product development. **Since** graduation, Oki's career has taken him to Minale Tattersfield in London via designing and lecturing in Ireland and Canada. On the way he has picked up a lot of different influences: he has particular respect for irish art and literature, for instance. But ancient Japanese culture forms the backbone of Oki's approach. 'Like the culture of Egypt,' he says, 'you don't know who did it but you know it's there.' **Minale Tattersfield's** newest partner is designer Nigel James Mac-Fall, a stalwart with the consultancy since 1978 who became partner in charge of interior design in January 1990. Mac-Fall once more brings impeccable credentials from the

Chairs
by Mario Bellini

Royal College of Art to Minale Tattersfield's creative frontline, but, importantly, he also brings a different perspective as the only partner trained specifically as a furniture designer. **He** believes that a furniture training – he studied first at Ravensbourne College of Art and Design and then at the RCA – is critical to the creation of successful, functioning interiors, and suggests that Minale Tattersfield's major scheme for Hammersmith Underground Station in London would not have been developed so inventively without having furniture designers on the team. '**Furniture** designers have an understanding of how structures go together,' explains Mac-Fall. 'The discipline is a marvellous grounding for almost any aspect of art and design. Why have all the classic furniture pieces been designed by architects? Because there is a clear relation between resolving the problems of a chair and a building'. **Mac-Fall** was given an early introduction to making structures: his father was an apprentice wheelwright in Scotland and was later involved in producing shopfitting in London. Mac-Fall even designed shopfronts as a teenager. As a schoolboy in Kent, he benefited from a special policy at Bromley Technical High school (run by the legendary Owen Frampton) which creamed off pupils gifted in art and design to spend three days a week studying the subject. Among his classmates were David Bowie and the illustrator Brian Grimwood. **Thus** Mac-Fall was introduced to the work of the

Bauhaus and the De Stijl art and architecture movement while still at school. De Stijl furniture designer Gerrit Rietveld (1888-1964) – creator of the famous Red-Blue chair of 1918 – was an early influence. Later Mac-Fall studied the work of Denmark's Poul Kjaerholm and Germany's Dieter Rams, who augmented domestic appliance design for Braun with a technically perfect shelving system for Swiss manufacturer Vitsoe. **At** the RCA, his tutor Ron Carter of Miles Carter – one of Britain's most consistently talented furniture designers – proved influential in stimulating his interest in the structural properties of materials in furniture. Mac-Fall's first jobs as a post graduate were at Planning Unit, where he worked on product development, and at the PSA where he spent three years designing the general issue office furniture for the Civil Service. 'Every time there's a TV news report from a government building, my furniture haunts me in the background,' laughs Mac-Fall. **His** time at Minale Tattersfield has combined architectural interiors and all types of three dimensional design. Not surprisingly he admits to being greatly influenced by architect Norman Foster's 1986 Nomos furniture range for Tecno. 'I enjoy the architectural influence on furniture,' says Mac-Fall. **Apart** from Nigel James Mac-Fall and Nobuoki Ohtani, other partners have come into the Minale Tattersfield group, each with their own ideas and influences. But the combined contribution of Minale, Tattersfield,

Nomos table
by Foster Associates

Grindle, Maranzano, Ohtani and Mac-Fall remains at the core of the group's creative direction.

Will Minale Tattersfield's work stand the test of time in the way that the designs of Robert Adam or Raymond Loewy or the Bauhaus have influenced successive generations of designers? That process is already happening. Of course one cannot legislate for centuries in the same way as decades, but the group has established a strong legacy in design, which draws on a marvellous array of cultural influences which cannot be ignored. Judge for yourself on these pages.

1986	**Dover Harbour Board**
1988	**NatWest Bank**
1990	**Hammersmith station**
1990	**Heathrow Express**

travel & **leisure**

1988	**Camera bag**
1980	**Ski goggles**
1972	**Heathrow subways**
1967	**Alitalia**
1981	**BAA exhibition poster**
1990	**Gatwick Village**
1982	**Taste exhibition**
1989	**Imperial War Museum**
1986	**London Zoo**
1990	**Manchester Olympic Bid**
1989	**Hangover Golf Society**

1

A fool wanders far, a wise man travels'
(Proverb)

DOVER

It is a familiar problem – and a tough one. Take an identity rich in historical tradition and up-date it for modern expectations without losing that enduring element of heraldry. The Port of Dover was one of the original 12th century cinque ports of England. Minale Tattersfield has given Dover, now one of the UK's busiest sea terminals for both passengers and freight, a new identity which integrates the original Cinque Ports lion-and-ship symbol with a graphic representation of the white cliffs of Dover. A simple, strong typeface underlines the adept transition to modernity.

The new identity has been successfully implemented throughout the Port's activities – from van liveries and uniforms to stationery. The Dover Harbour Board Police have even used the new image as part of their own identity.

Good ideas are universal, none more so than in this brochure for
NatWest's Travel Service which was designed in the form of a fold-out
travel map. The palm tree emblem on the front is created from the
familiar topography of relief map graphics. This theme is picked up
inside with the Eiffel Tower and Leaning Tower of Pisa rendered in the
same way.

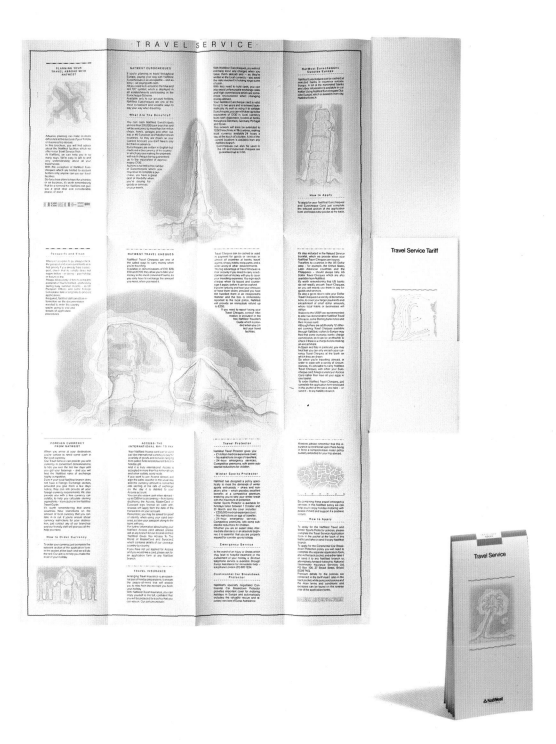

Most stations on the
London Underground
network are buried
deep below ground.
But Hammersmith Station
is out in the open.
Minale Tattersfield was
commissioned in 1989 to
redesign the station as part
of a major new development.
The confusing nature of the
site called for a scheme
which would unite the visual
elements, create a unique
sense of place, evoke the
best traditions of London
Transport design and
provide shelter for
passengers while retaining
an airy, open environment.

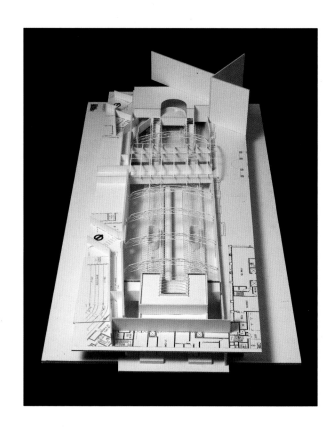

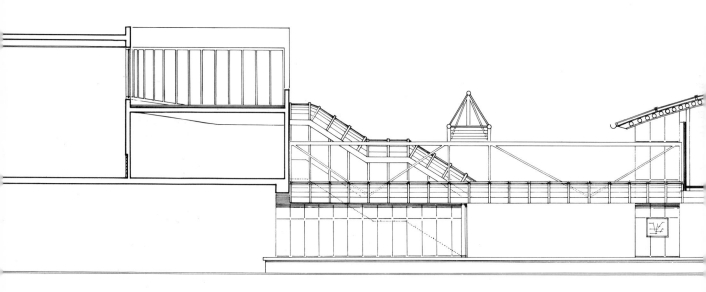

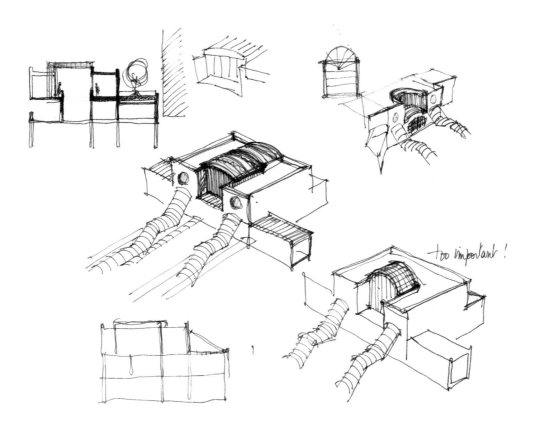

too important !

Project
Hammersmith Station

Client
London Underground

Address

Date	Scale
06 10 89	**1/ 100**
Job No.	**Sheet No.**
7526	**02**

Title
Design Concept
North Ticket Hall and Bridges

Minale, Tattersfield & Partners Limited
The Courtyard, 37 Sheen Road, Richmond, Surrey TW9 1AJ
Telephone: 01-948 7999 Telex: 22397 MINTAT G Fax 01-948 2435

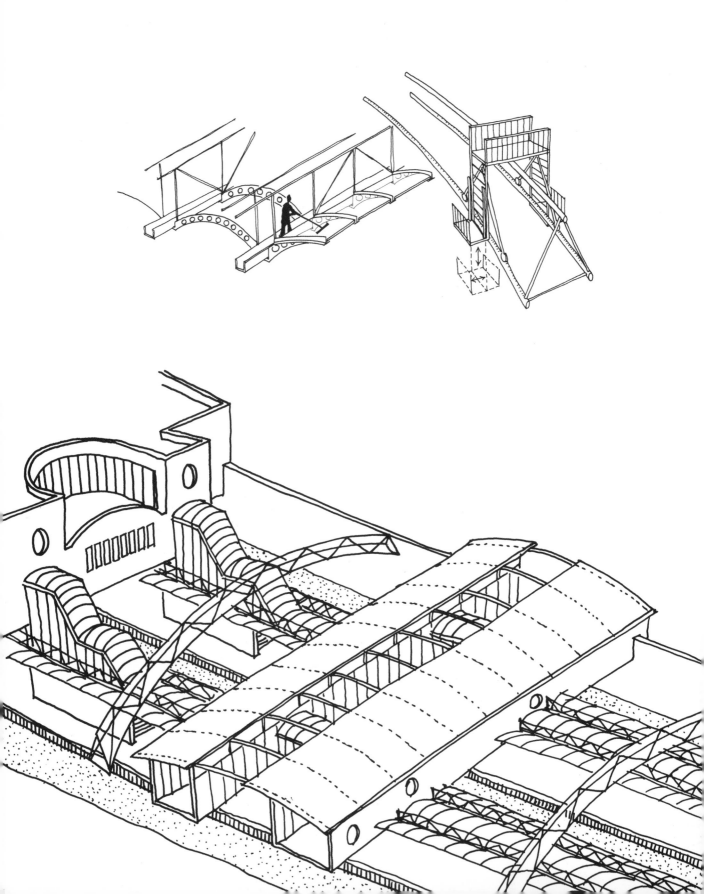

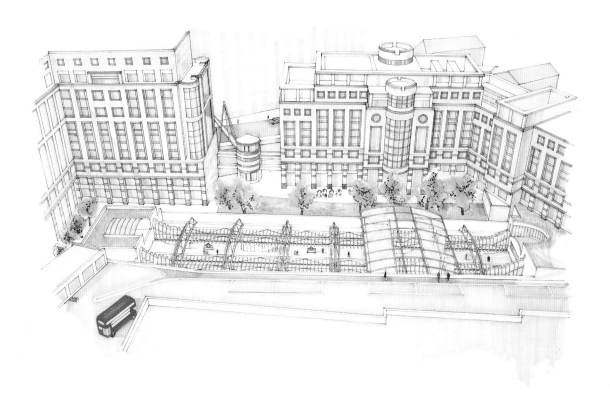

The entire station area at Hammersmith has been spanned by a series of lattice beams, so clearing the platforms of structural columns and organising the space with a broad simplicity. The beams, from which the canopies sheltering the station are suspended, have integrated catwalks and cradles for easy maintenance. The central arched section of the canopy acts as a roof to the waiting rooms and kiosks on the platforms. On either side of this arch run large gutters painted in the 'line' colours of the station, effectively combining decoration and function. Despite the site's complexity, the directness of the solution demonstrates Minale Tattersfield's belief that when design is not over-elaborate, it has the power to solve a many-faceted problem.

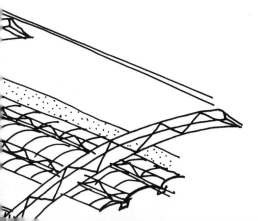

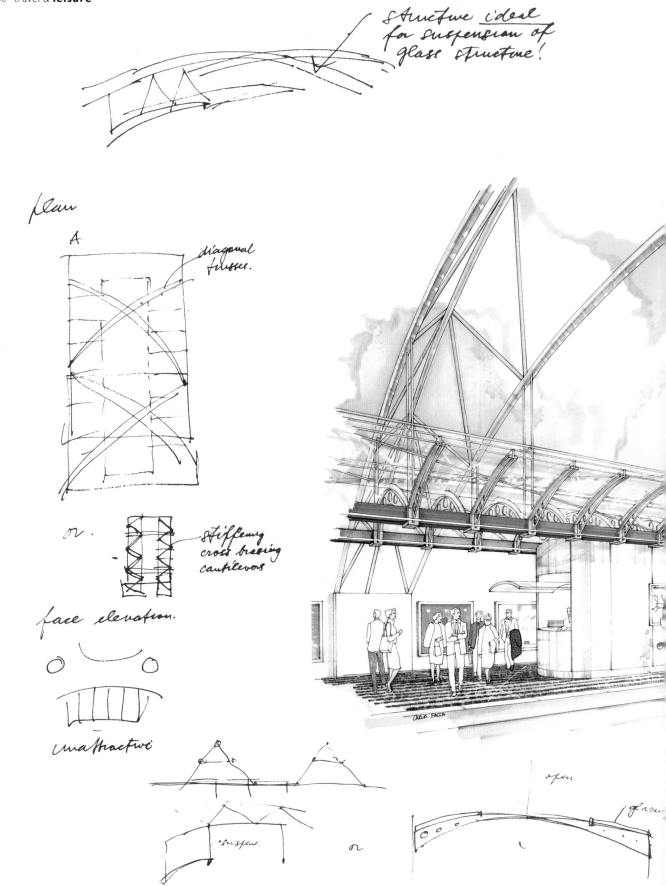

Structure ideal for suspension of glass structure!

plan

A

diagonal trusses.

or.

stiffening cross bracing cantilevers

face elevation.

unattractive

suspen.

or

open

glazing

CARLA FACCIA

purpose of structure?

wind driven
rain.

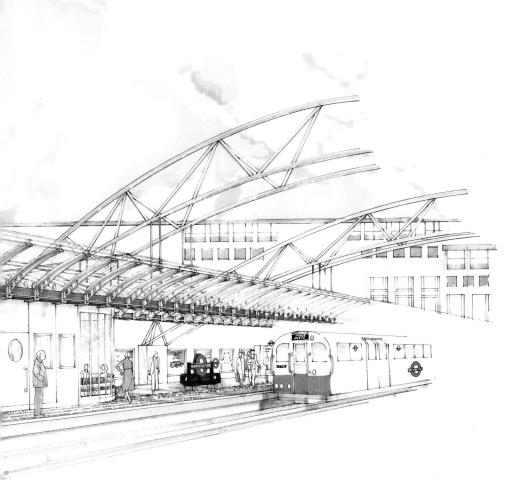

Hammersmith station platform area,
showing glass and enamel kiosks with
interlocking concrete paving.

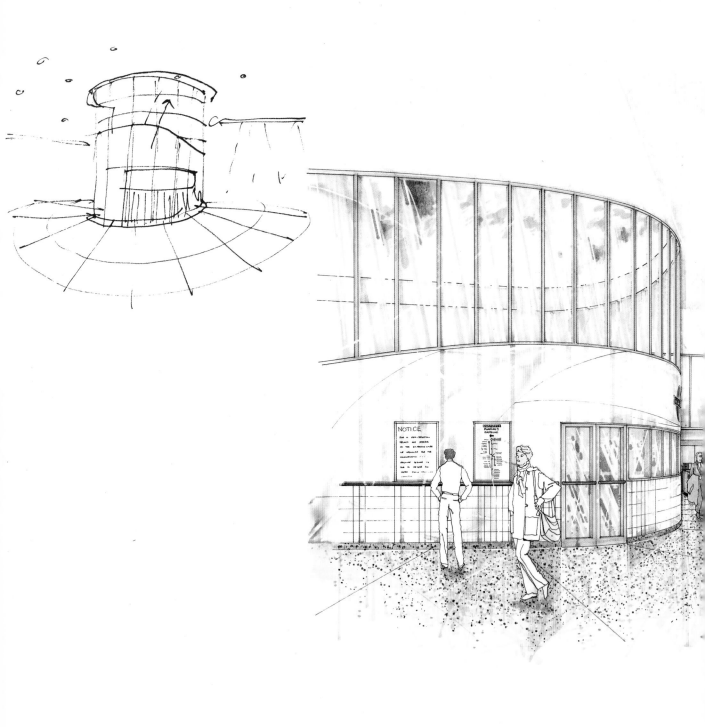

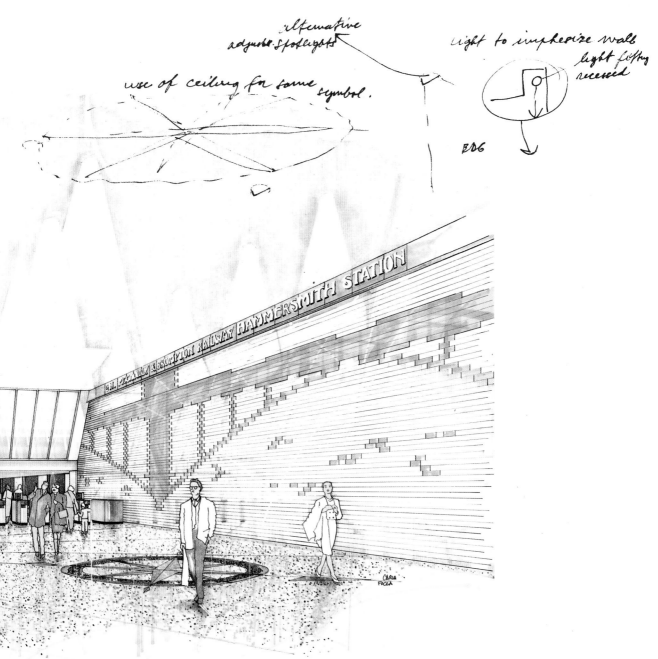

Hammersmith station ticket hall, including original ceramic frieze above 'reflection' of Hammersmith Bridge.

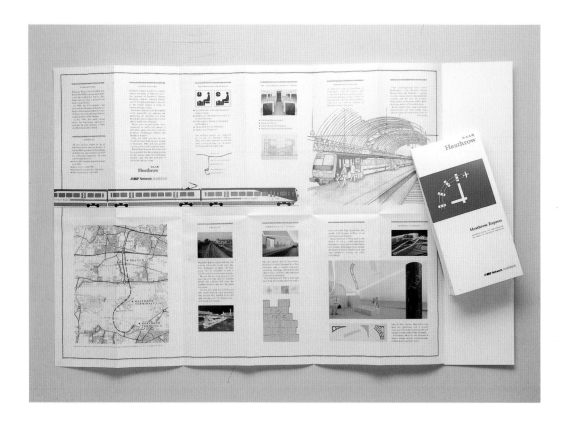

Heathrow Express is a new high-speed rail service which will link Paddington with Heathrow Airport in just 16 minutes. It is scheduled to start operating in 1993 and Minale Tattersfield is taking a major role in its development, working on both train livery and interior design, graphics and station environments. This foldout leaflet explains the key elements of the scheme. The Heathrow Express symbol cleverly reflects the idea that the journey time is around a quarter of an hour and that trains leave every 15 minutes. The graphic representations of industrial ironwork are from proposals for the station at terminal 4.

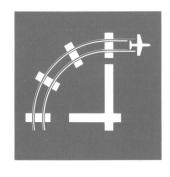

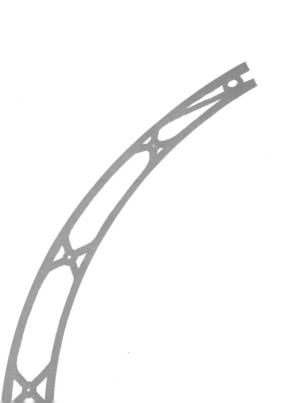

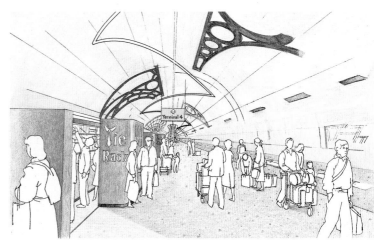

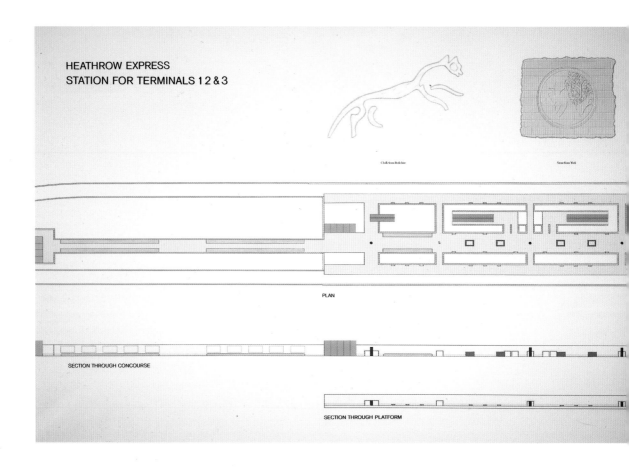

HEATHROW EXPRESS
STATION FOR TERMINALS 1 2 & 3

Chalk from Berkshire

Staunton on Vale

PLAN

SECTION THROUGH CONCOURSE

SECTION THROUGH PLATFORM

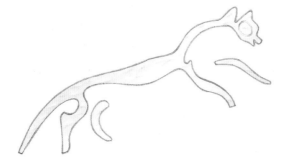

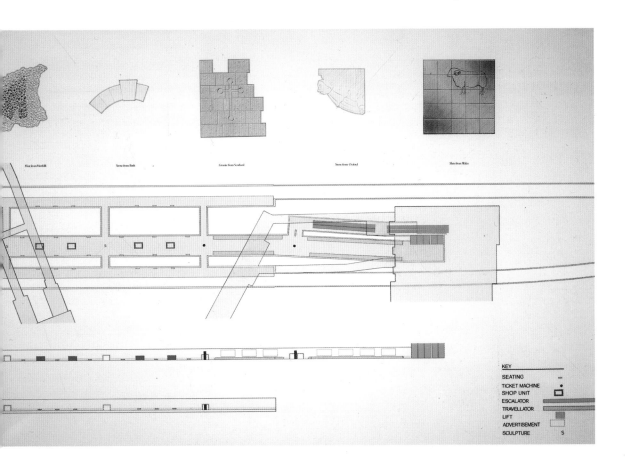

Flint from Norfolk   Stone from Bath   Granite from Scotland   Stone from Oxford   Slate from Wales

KEY

SEATING	—
TICKET MACHINE	•
SHOP UNIT	☐
ESCALATOR	
TRAVELLATOR	
LIFT	
ADVERTISEMENT	
SCULPTURE	S

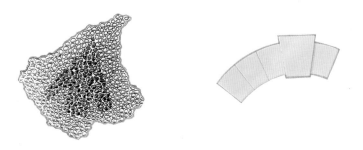

Proposals for other stations at Heathrow focus on traditional British '-ologies': palaeontology, archaeology, geology and architecture (sic).

To convey proposed designs
for the Heathrow Express
train, Minale Tattersfield
worked with photographer
Ken Kirkwood to create the
right effect using block
models and photo-montage.
The train's appearance is
based on working the shape
of Concorde into the livery
to symbolise aerodynamic
speed and excitement.
Colours also relate to the
corporate identity of BAA,
which is partnering British
Rail in developing the new
Paddington-Heathrow link.
The image of Concorde
flying above the new
Heathrow Express has
worked effectively in a
wide variety of promotional
contexts.

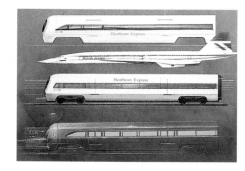

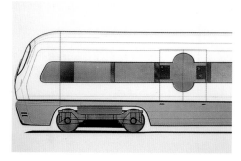

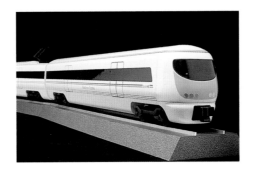

Interior proposals for the Heathrow Express train emphasise convenience, comfort and safety. Wide doors, non-slip floors, large luggage racks and simple information panels make life easier for passengers on the move. One telephone per carriage is envisaged, plus ample provision for the disabled. A proposal to use self-folding theatre-style seating may prove too costly, but the idea works so well in terms of access, maintenance and security (suspicious parcels will be noticed) that it should be shown anyway..

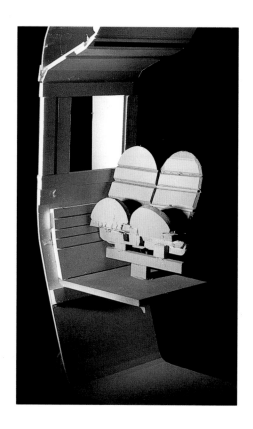

The Steelgranite Bench, which will be used on the Heathrow Express project, has been developed by Minale Tattersfield to combat the three perennial problems of design for public places: dirt, deterioration and vandalism. Produced by Zoeftig, it is made of rolled, perforated stainless steel with mild steel arms and concrete composite legs – the latter making it simple to clean around.

Canadian Mountain Equipment camera bags are aimed at the semi-professional market where ergonomic design matters. Shaped to fit body contours, the bags offer easy access for the user as they open away from the body.

Functional yet striking, these economically-styled goggles don't have a conventional frame. Instead there is a large screen made of injection-moulded polycarbonate, with foam cushioning and a stretchable fabric strap which is wide enough to keep the ears warm.

A commission to decorate the lengthy passenger subways at Heathrow Airport, which link the scattered termini, called for graphic ingenuity to make these tunnels less claustrophobic.

Among the ideas: a dove which takes off when you step onto the travellator, flies along beside you and lands when you get off. Overleaf, an A to Z of foreign and domestic destinations.

from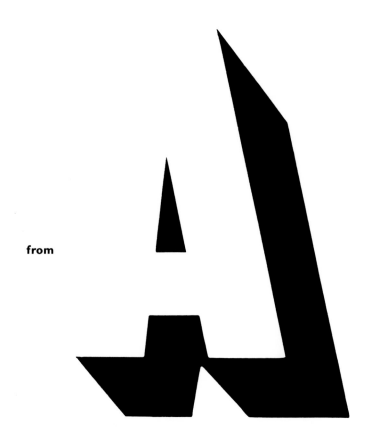

ASCOTBATHCAERNARVONDOVEREDINBURGHFARNBOROUGHGREENWICHHASTINGSILKLEYJARROWKILMARNOCKLONDONMON

AMSTERDAMBANGKOKCOPENHAGENDUSSELDORFESTORILFAMAGUSTAGENEVAHELSINKIISTANBULJERICHOKIEVLEIPZIG

to

RWICHOXFORDPOOLEQUEENSBORORICHMONDSHEFFIELDTORQUAYUCKFIELDVENTNORWINCHESTERXANADUYORKZENNOR

EONAIROBIOSLOPARISQUEBECROMESHANGHAITIPPERARYUPPSALAVIENNAWASHINGTONXANTHIYOKOHAMAZAGREB

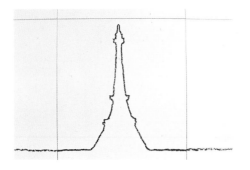

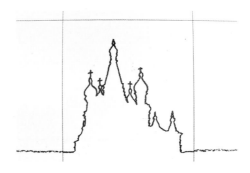

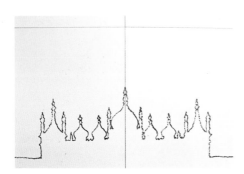

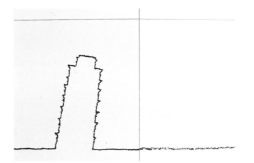

As with the A to Z design, this graffiti-style
graphic echoes the incoming-outgoing
theme: British sights like Brighton for
arrivals and foreign landmarks like the
Pyramids for departures.

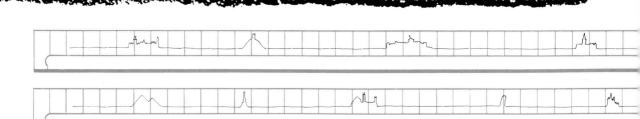

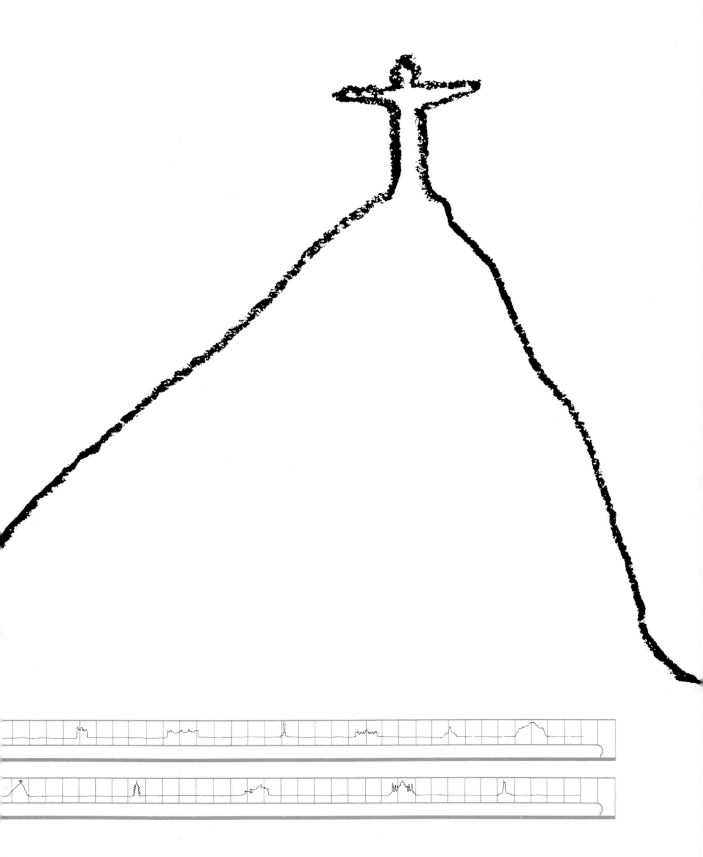

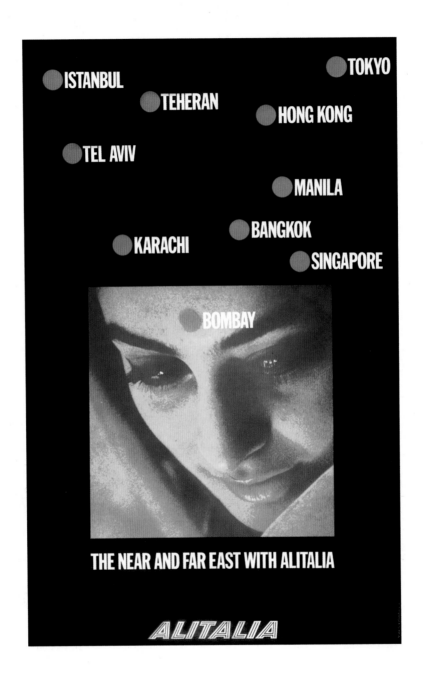

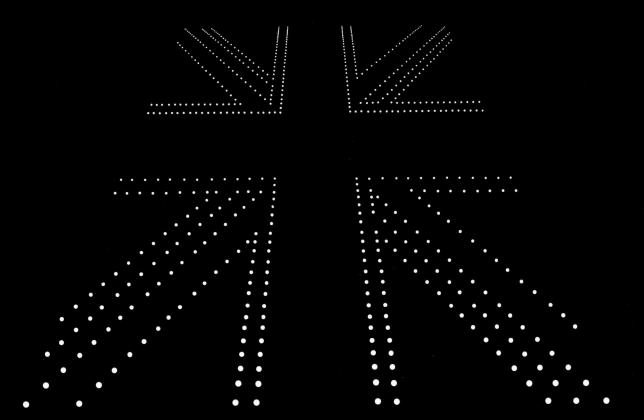

British Airports at The Design Centre

Haymarket, London. June 19 – July 21. Open Monday – Saturday 09.30 – 17.30. Wednesday & Thursday until 21.00. Admission free

GATWICK VILLAGE

A new identity for Gatwick Village – an upper level complex in the airport which incorporates shops, restaurants, bars and buffets. The letters of the logo are made up from information symbols, the shopping bag reference in the 'L' pointing travellers in the right direction. Classically, the solution has been found in the problem – the identity is the signage and vice versa.

One of the most controversial design exhibitions of the 1980s, 'Taste' (a Boilerhouse Project at the Victoria & Albert Museum) certainly encouraged argument. Minale Tattersfield created an 'island' setting for each of the exhibition's eight sections, mounted objects in good taste on white plinths and those in bad taste on dustbins, then lit the blue touch-paper...

IMPERIAL WAR MUSEUM

The Imperial War Museum, once described as 'the biggest boy's bedroom in London', has undergone a dramatic architectural refurbishment. Minale Tattersfield's role was to create a new visual identity for an institution displaying the history of military and civilian conflict from 1914 to the present day. The chosen solution – in which searchlights form the initials 'WM' against a background of land, sea and sky – has a starkness which avoids the glorification of war.

War-time visual archaeology: spot the
origins of the letters, e.g. the 'O' from the
American Mustang's star symbol.

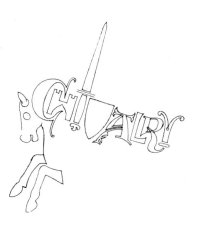

The Age of Chivalry, the largest-ever art exhibition staged at the Royal Academy, was sponsored by Lloyds Bank. Minale Tattersfield took the famous Lloyds prancing horse symbol as the basis for a logo which expressed the theme and content of the exhibition. The lettering was composed from medieval fragments drawn from manuscripts and architectural elements of Plantagenet England. This literal interpretation was then extended across a range of promotional material.

One of the older schemes in the Minale Tattersfield portfolio but still a great favourite: the Café at London Zoo in Regent's Park enlivened by a series of brightly coloured hanging signs. All the animals in the sign series are incorporated into a clock with knife-and-fork hands.

THE CAFÉ IN THE ZOO

Creatures depicted at the café in the zoo are drawn from primitive art.

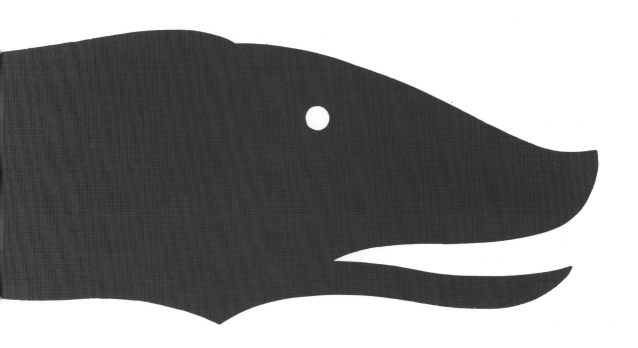

ADOPT AN ANIMAL

Logo for campaign to
persuade the public to
'adopt an animal'.

Manchester is making the official British bid to host the 1996 Olympic Games. The Manchester Olympic Bid Committee commissioned Minale Tattersfield to create an identity to support its effort. The brief was far from straightforward: two separate logos were required, one for use by the bid committee itself (incorporating the existing British Olympic Committee symbol of five Olympic rings and the Union Jack) and another for sponsors to use on their products.

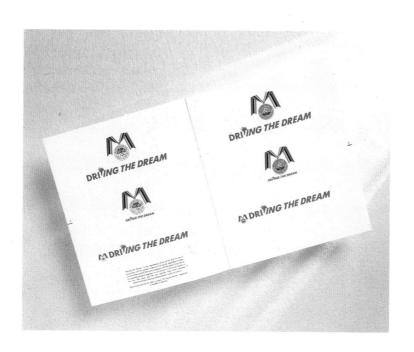

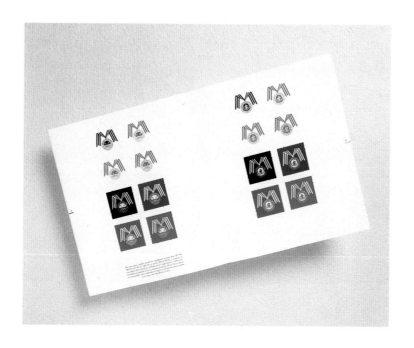

Part of the promotional task was to encourage local enthusiasm for the Olympic bid. These posters push the 'British' message home, wittily using famous figures to conjure up that characteristically British combination of amateur enthusiasm, patriotic determination and genuine sportsmanship.

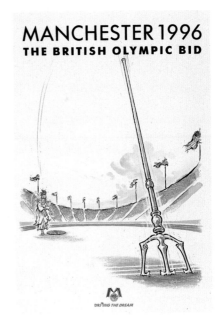

Meanwhile, more seriously, a comprehensive pack of information and promotional material (including the book shown overleaf) was assembled and presented to the International Olympic Committee before their visit to Manchester in September 1990. The colours of the M-shaped braided closures are echoed in the design of the contents.

As part of Manchester's Olympic bid, Minale Tattersfield designed a 150 page publication to attract the Olympics to the north-west of England. The story outlines the sporting traditions of the region and colourfully illustrates exactly how Manchester and Britain would go about staging such an important series of events.

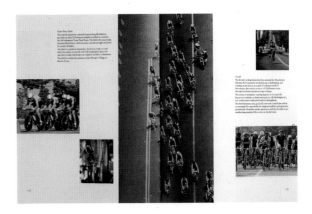

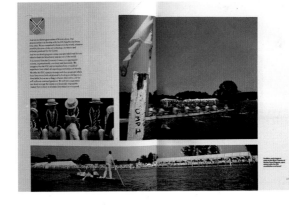

You are cordially invited to join us for drinks at the inaugural meeting of the Hangover Golf Society, 8.30 pm, Saturday 6th May 1989 at Sunningdale Gol

RSVP, Anne Wilson, Princeton House, Osiers Road, London SW18.

Designed by Minale Tattersfield & Partners

A visual variation on the nineteenth hole. The Hangover Golfing Society is a sporting organisation with the accent on the social, set up by Minale Tattersfield client Princeton Developments. This poster promotes one of its events. Don't bet on the members managing to sink the putt, though.

"So|

Tennis tuition

Apply to the Secretary, Brentham Tennis Cl

ry!"

or beginners

Meadvale Road, Ealing W 5 Tel 01-997 2624

1988 **The Workers Scribble**

1989 **Princeton**

1990 **Christies**

commercial & **industrial**

1978 **Jewson**

1987 **Alesco**

1989 **Buckingham Gate**

1987 **ISIS**

1987 **HB Signs**

1987 **Industrial Scribble**

1972 **Zanotta table**

1986 **Parmesan chair**

1989 **British Petroleum**

1989 **Toyota**

2

'Life without industry is
guilt, and industry
without art is brutality'
(John Ruskin)

"THE WORKERS"

(Around 25,000)

PRINCETON
P L C   G R O U P

1988 Annual Report

PRINCETON
DEVELOPMENTS

Often the simplest ideas in identity work the best. This symbol for a building company reflects the nature of the business and its prospects for future growth by using a neat typographical device: the letter 'D' which emerges from the centre of the letter 'P' simulates a building rising from its foundations. The new symbol, which has been adapted for use within other divisions of the Princeton group, has also been incorporated into each page of the annual report in the form of a faint background tint. The annual report (opposite page) was laid out on a grid system similar to architectural plans, thus extending the design theme.

There's no business like repeat business. Following the success of the Princeton identity, Minale Tattersfield was approached again by the client to create a new image for its latest acquisition, estate agent and property consultant Christies. Using the old saying 'An Englishman's home is his castle', the consultancy drew a moat around the castle to create the 'C' of Christies. The heraldic theme was developed further by designing colour-coded property boards in the shape of shields. Green signifies under offer, red for sale, and black sold. Christies is an old-established business founded in 1938. Its colourful new identity provided Princeton with the springboard to develop it into a major chain covering the property market in the South East.

The logo for timber and building merchants Jewson is underlined by a carpenter's rule which acts as a general device on stationery and in showrooms. Not only was the project implemented in just over two months, but the solution proved durable in a market in which a more precious solution would not have survived.

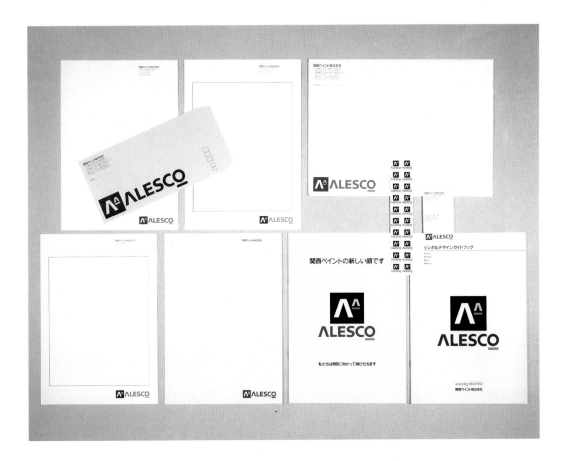

Alesco – a brand created for Japanese chemical and paint firm, Kansai – had to communicate safety and stability while also reflecting the company's corporate slogan: 'to advance with people and technology'. The name actually means 'to grow up' in Latin and the final emblem is in the style of a chemical symbol.

This symbol for a
Charter plc development at
66 Buckingham Gate echoes
the wrought iron scrollwork
common to the St. James's
area – the gates of the Palace
itself are a good example.

Smaller projects can often stretch the creative boundaries. This range of stationery
for an industrial design consultancy called ISIS prompted a play on the name, illustrating
ices as though they were industrial designs. This witty idea of using technically drawn
foodstuffs was not as far-fetched as it appeared: for instance, the great Italian car
designer Giorgio Guigaro went on to produce technical drawing when creating his own
aerodynamic pasta shells. Nevertheless, it was a case of asking the client to suck it and see.

This promotional mailer for a sign company is an old favourite which still looks fresh. The MSS 0.5 Modular Sign System by HB signs is aimed squarely at architects and designers at the top end of the market. The mailer leads you through a building, demonstrating as you go the type sizes and colours available in the range.

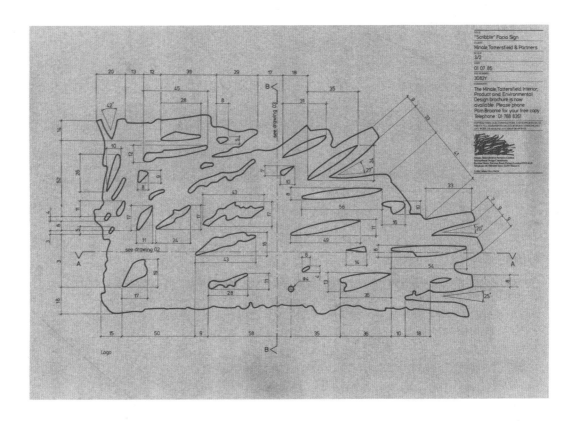

The famous Minale Tattersfield scribble logo, memorably rendered in technical style, as a three-dimensional symbol to promote the consultancy's interior, environmental and product design expertise…

Minale Tattersfield's work with famous Italian furniture company Zanotta produced a variety of forms over the years. This knock-down table added quality and style to spacesaving furniture. Made out of seven solid wood leg pieces and a practical laminate top, it can be constructed or collapsed in seconds. Simple, stable and sturdy, you can store it and transport it flat with ease. A marvellous example of function enhancing (or, indeed, creating) beauty, this table is used by Marcello Minale as his desk to this day.

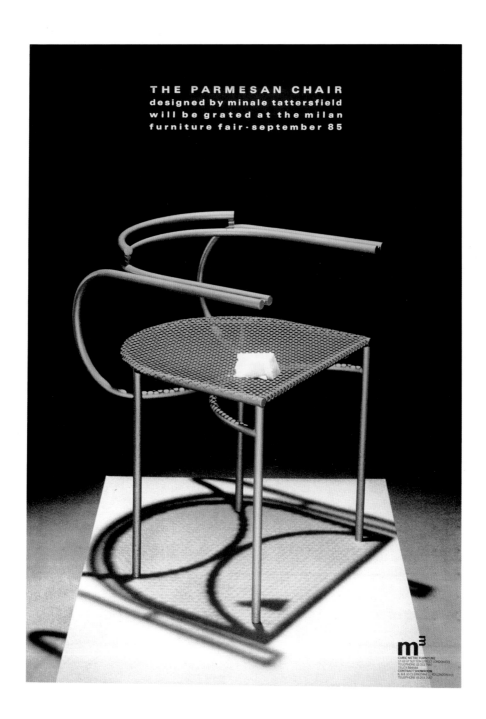

Perceptions of Minale Tattersfield as a consultancy primarily renowned for the witty solution in visual communication were dramatically revised by the success of a major technical packaging programme for BP oil. The in-depth, international nature of the project – which called for a complete reappraisal of the image and performance of the petrol station forecourt oil can – tested the consultancy's design development facilities to the full. **Initial** research revealed that a marked decline in the demand for motor oil (due to more efficient cars requiring less servicing) was accompanied by a bewildering array of budget-priced oil cans for sale. Furthermore, motorists complained that oil cans – often made of the cheapest varieties of tin-plate and plastic – were ugly, uncomfortable, messy and sometimes dangerous to use. In response, a series of prototypes was produced.

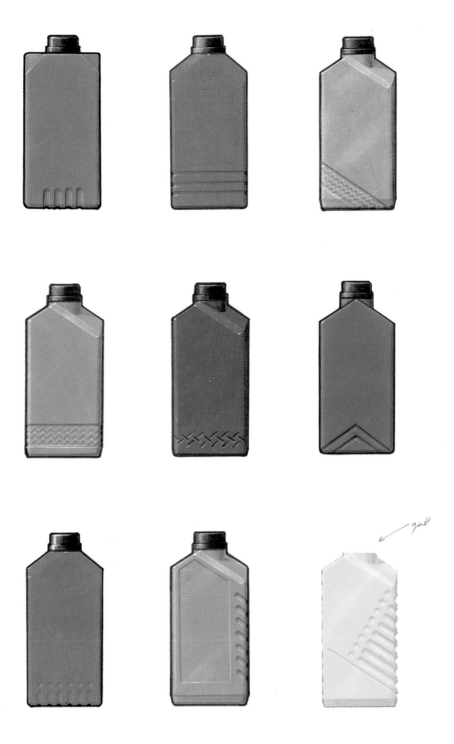

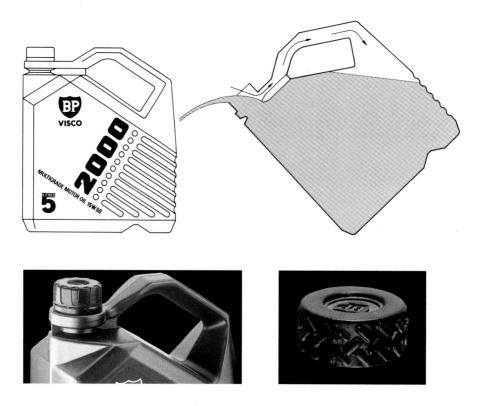

There were two major problems with traditional oil packs. First, many packs – especially large ones – were difficult to handle and pour, especially under a car bonnet. Second, they were bedevilled by 'glugging', which disrupts the flow of oil and causes spillage as uncontrolled air rushes into the pack body as oil flows out slowly through the narrow neck. The solution was the 'Easy Flow System', a piece of technical ingenuity which comprises a unique 'anti-glug' restrictor in the neck of the pack. This both stabilises the oil flow out and controls the rush of air in, thus eliminating glugging altogether.

Ease of handling was achieved by giving the packs a low and stable centre of gravity. A special reversible grip was developed for the one-litre pack, so providing the same gripping characteristics for left and right-handed people. The five-litre pack was given an in-built finger grip in the bottom of the pack to make handling easier. In addition, the reversible design offered production benefits: with identical faces, it no longer mattered which way they presented themselves on the production line.

The new oil packs – ranging from 500ml to five litres – were put into exhaustive market research and findings confirmed the choice of colours: a silvery green for the premium grade, a moss green for the mid-range, and a matt yellow for the economy grade. Gold, silver and black, the archetypal choice for traditional oil cans, had become clichéd in the eyes of motorists, for whom the aerodynamic shape of the new BP packaging reflected current and future trends in car styling. **Once** more, Minale Tattersfield had proved itself one step ahead of the game. As for BP, an interlocking array of production, distribution, product image, performance and segmentation problems had been masterfully resolved. The new packaging is now in use in more than 20 countries around the world and BP is now, in the words of Marcello Minale, 'ten years ahead of the competition'.

Synthetic oil is the oil of the future: it preserves natural resources and is better for your engine.

This new range of oils gives BP the chance to look at still more radical pack shapes. This time the theme is the cylinder block – where oil is needed most and worked hardest. **Four** initial concepts appear here: they range from designs similar to BP's international oil range (q.v) to more radical ones like the piston-shaped design with a peel-off replaceable strip. With this and the more angular slab-sided design, there will be two holes beneath the strip, one to pour and the other to allow air in to prevent 'glugging'. **All** the designs are in blow-moulded plastic and are still very much at the prototype stage. Nevertheless, the packs – like the oil itself – are definitely the shape of things to come.

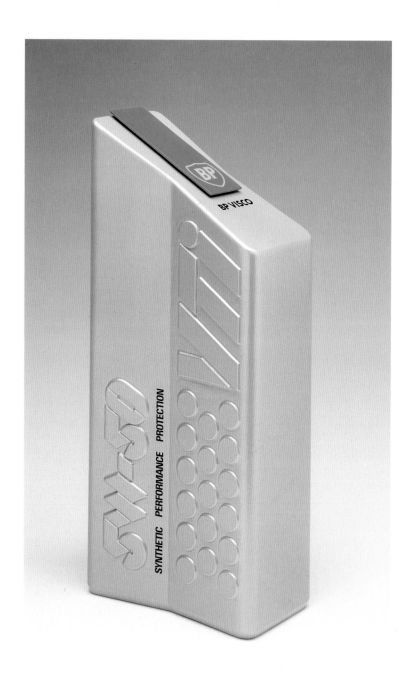

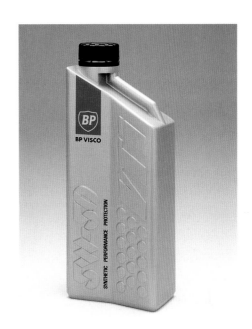

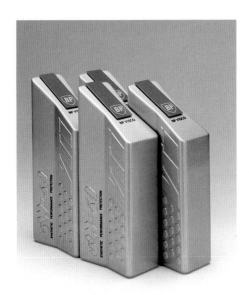

When Toyota of Japan decided to redesign its corporate identity, it selected ten top international design groups from around the world to submit proposals. Three groups were shortlisted, among them Minale Tattersfield. Shown here are examples of the development work which went into the pitch for Toyota. In the event, the car maker chose to go with Japanese design group Nippon Design. Minale Tattersfield had narrowly missed the marque …

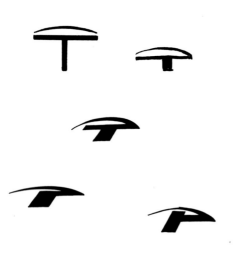

The one that got away (incidentally bearing
an uncanny resemblance to the Nippon
Design solution which Toyota eventually
chose) …

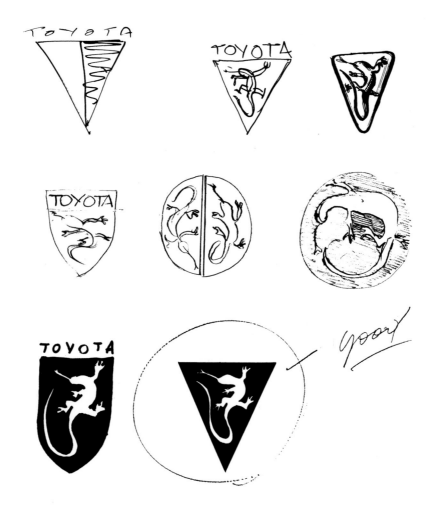

An alternative proposal – à la Ferrari,
Porsche, Lamborghini and Jaguar – also
slithered away …

1987 **Post Office stamps**

Christmas cards

1981 **Design & Art Direction**

publishing & **media**

1989 **Best of British Corporate**

1988 **Best of British Packaging**

1989 **Parkway**

1980 **Central**

1960 **American in Paris**

1989 **The Visual Team**

1976 **24 Wrong Ideas**

3

'What you see is news,
what you know is
background, what you feel
is opinion'
(New York Times)

British architects have designed some of the most significant recent buildings in Europe – a fact celebrated in a set of commemorative stamps commissioned by the Post Office for the Conference of European Posts and Telecommunications (CEPT). **The** 'British Architects in Europe' series was developed by Minale Tattersfield by building model representations of the buildings and photographing them. The results proved intriguing and engaging. **Featured** buildings are the Willis Faber and Dumas headquarters in Ipswich (Norman Foster), the Pompidou Centre in Paris (Richard Rogers with Renzo Piano), the Staatsgalerie in Stuttgart (James Stirling) and the European Investment Bank in Luxembourg (Denys Lasdun). The consultancy also designed a range of supporting material.

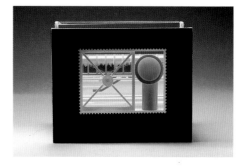

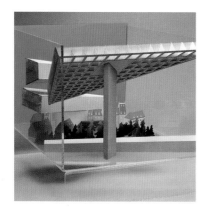

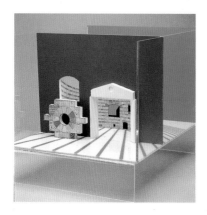

ROYAL MAIL SPECIAL STAMPS:

BRITISH ARCHITECTS IN EUROPE

FOUR SPECIAL STAMPS TO BE ISSUED ON:
TUESDAY 12 MAY 1987

Mrs J Robinson
200 Manorbier Road
ILKESTON
Derbyshire
DE7 4AB

The Postmark shown here is available only from the British Philatelic Bureau

ROYAL MAIL FIRST DAY COVER ON SALE NOW UNTIL:	PRICE:
12 MAY 1987	16P (ENVELOPE AND FILLER CARD ONLY)

BRITISH ARCHITECTS IN EUROPE
ROYAL MAIL MINT STAMPS

PRESENTATION PACK ON SALE FROM:	PRICE:
12 MAY 1987	£1.27

18P
BRITISH ARCHITECTS IN EUROPE
FOSTER
IPSWICH

POSTCARDS ON SALE NOW PRICE:
15P EACH (POSTAGE EXTRA)

It may be the mulled wine but the promotional opportunities at Christmas tend to enable the consultancy to pull the wittiest ideas out of the cracker. Shown here are some family favourites: the famous Minale Tattersfield scribble depicted as a winter sky; a roll of film transformed into a party blower for photographer Ken Kirkwood; Cubic Metre table lamps strung together to form Christmas tree lights…

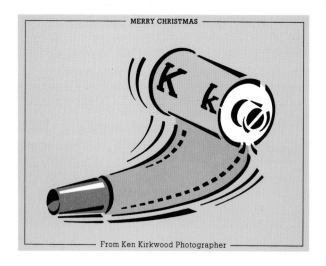

MERRY CHRISTMAS

From Ken Kirkwood Photographer

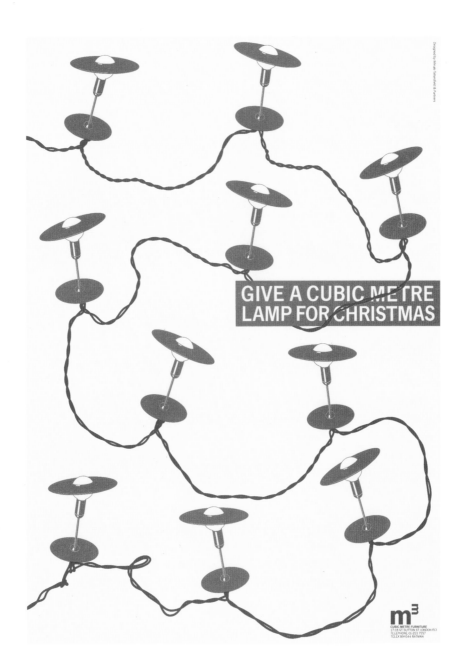

GIVE A CUBIC METRE
LAMP FOR CHRISTMAS

m³

CUBIC METRE FURNITURE
17-18 GT SUTTON ST LONDON EC1
TELEPHONE 01-253 7557
TELEX 894544 BATMAN

m³

CHRISTMAS GREETINGS FROM CUBIC METRE FURNITURE

Charlotte & Jeff
CHRISTMAS
LØNTOFTEN 17, 3070 SNEKKERSTEN DANMARK
TLF: 02·22 25 25

Cubic Metre Furniture

Minale Tattersfield, Design Strategy

Crown Suppliers

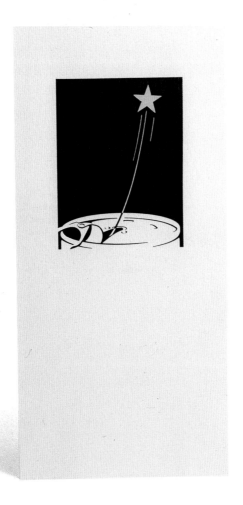

San Pellegrino soft drinks.

CALL FOR ENTRIES
THE GRAPHIC WORKSHOP
SPONSORED BY THE DESIGNERS & ART DIRECTORS ASSOCIATION

The Graphic Workshop once again provides the opportunity, instruction and creative atmosphere for exciting experiment in visual communication and seeks participants who are students, art school graduates or those who have had equivalent experience. The Workshop is highly selective in its choice of members and the number of participants is necessarily limited so that discussion and criticism may be intense. Applicants must submit portfolios of their work, together with their name and address. These must be brought to the Design & Art Directors Association Office, 3rd Floor, Nash House, 12 Carlton House Terrace, London SW1Y 5AH, not later than 5.30 pm on **17 October 1984,** and will be reviewed by the Selection Committee the following day. Applicants will be notified by post whether or not they have been accepted for the Workshop. The D & AD will not be responsible for work not collected by 5.30 pm on 22 October 1984. There will be five sessions of the Workshop on the evenings of 22, 29 October and 5, 13, 19 November 1984 from 6.30 to 9.00 pm at the SIAD, 1st Floor, 12 Carlton House Terrace, London SW1Y 5AH. There will be a £25.00 fee payable in advance.

PEEL BACKING TO EXPOSE ADHESIVE

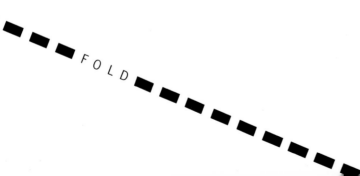

F O L D

In 1987 the Designers and Art Directors Association (D&AD) presented
Marcello Minale and Brian Tattersfield with the prestigious President's
Award for outstanding contribution to design. A fitting tribute, given the
consultancy's efforts in supporting the development of D&AD and
designing many examples of its literature.

MADE IN GREAT BRITAIN

The Best of British Corporate Design is a compilation volume edited by Edward Booth-Clibborn and published by Booth-Clibborn Editions. Minale Tattersfield designed the book with a front cover image suggesting the targeting of identities to achieve maximum impact.

Another collaboration between Minale Tattersfield and Edward Booth-Clibborn, The Best of British Packaging has a special medal motif suspended from a bar-code ribbon, which is used on the front cover and throughout the book.

PARKWAY GROUP PLC

The enigmatic imagery of the magician
performing the famous never-ending scarf
trick is a bold and imaginative way to sum
up the Parkway Group in a new corporate
identity. The client – whose international
pre-press production service extends from
the UK to America, France, Italy and
Germany – wanted a new image which
appealed to its predominantly advertising
agency client base, as well as financial
advisers and institutional investors.
This design encapsulates the exciting and
inspirational side of its business, which is
very much part of the creative industry.

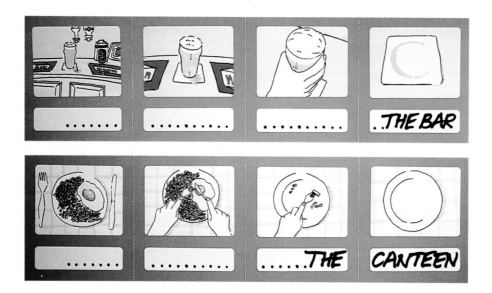

..THE BAR

.....THE CANTEEN

Today we are faced with a plethora of new television station identities as cable and satellite TV take hold. Some are imaginative, many are not. Against the new wave of TV station images, Minale Tattersfield's longstanding work for Central Television remains as fresh as ever. The sphere symbol has infinite application: for example, the front cover of the annual report portrays a total eclipse. Internal studio signs for bar and canteen, meanwhile, are rendered in the style of storyboards.

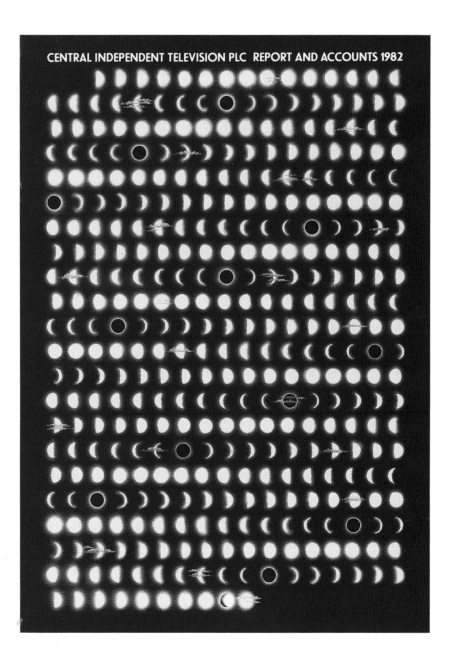

THE VISUAL TEAM

Minale Tattersfield's representative in Italy, The Visual Team, is the country's largest agency for illustrators and photographers. This new identity, devised after the company had been in business for a decade, uses a selection of differently-styled portraits to symbolise the wide spread of talent on The Visual Team's books.

24 wrong ideas from Minale Tattersfield

Client: Italian Institute for Foreign Trade
Problem: Promotion for Italian pears, oranges, grapes and peaches
Solution: An Italian apple

Having an idea is often like looking for a lost glove
and finding a lost sock.
After many years of getting good ideas for things
we were not meant to solve, we decided to keep a
record of this little sideline.
Here are a few of them:

Client: Italian Institute for Foreign Trade
Problem: Catalogue cover for exhibition of Italian footwear
Solution: Footwear festival in Cairo

Client: London Sinfonietta
Problem: Programme cover
Solution: Programme cover for Scottish national orchestra

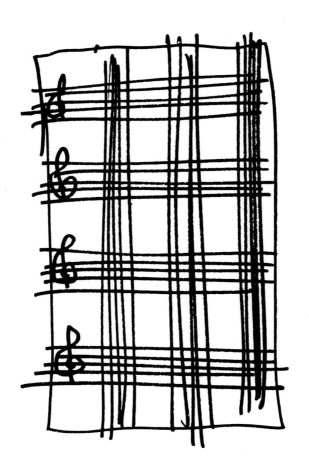

Client: Milton Keynes Development Corporation
Problem: Cover for a leaflet on overspill in the south east of England
Solution: Cover for a book entitled "Arrogance"

Client: Llewellyn-Davies
Problem: Symbol for international architects
Solution: Symbol for hospital architecture

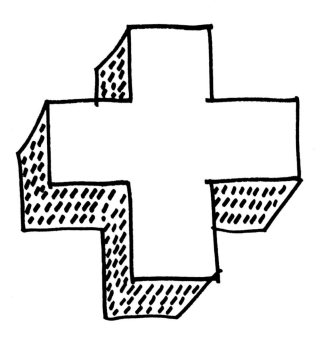

Client: Hospital Design Partnership

Once in a lifetime—if you're lucky—you get a
problem to a solution

1990   **Global Securities**

1987   **Financial Scribble**

1989   **NatWest Personal Loans**

banking & **finance**

1988   **NatWest Car Loans**

1986   **Gold Plus**

1989   **European Banking**

1988   **NatWest Calendar**

1989   **NatWest Calendar**

1990   **NatWest Calendar**

4

'Money is better than
poverty, if only for
financial reasons'
(Woody Allen)

NatWest's Global Securities Service required a professional-looking
pack to attract a highly sophisticated clientele for their international
custodial investment services. The fold-out globe, the encircling bank
names and the chain-link imagery represent the coverage and security
central to the GSS service.

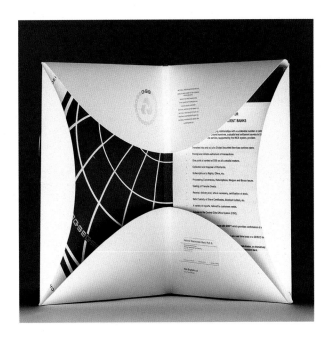

Minale Tattersfield has a wealth of
experience in the financial field – so much
so that they have their own financial
communications literature. The Scribble
logo adapted perfectly.

National Westminster Bank has been a Minale Tattersfield client for almost ten years. Much of the work created has been aimed at the everyday customer. Here, and overleaf, we find countertop posters graphically proclaiming the benefits of personal loans. The puns are intentional ...

NatWest Personal Loans

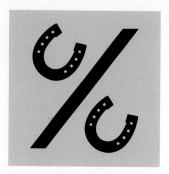

Stable interest

U3 12/88

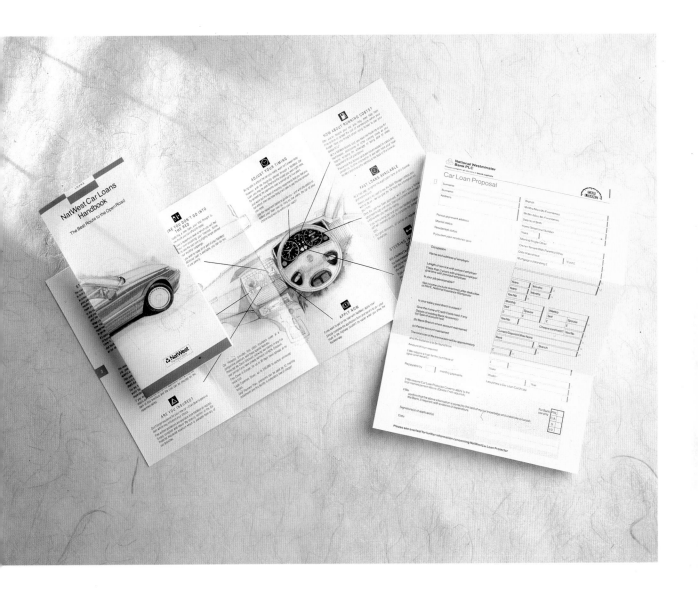

NatWest's Car Loans literature typifies the inventiveness which Minale Tattersfield has consistently brought to financial communications. It is based on the concept of the car handbook with the car loans application form in the style of an official vehicle registration form.

NatWest Car Loans

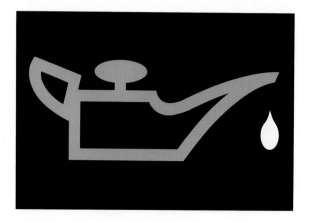

SMOOTH YOUR TRANSACTIONS

The Action Bank

WS CP CL 8 4/89

Key points in the NatWest Car Loans
brochure are illustrated by familiar symbols
taken from a car's dashboard. These also
adapt for use on large display posters and
panels.

NatWest Car Loans

KEEP A CLEAR VIEW

&NatWest
The Action Bank

NatWest Car Loans

GAUGE YOUR FINANCES

&NatWest
The Action Bank

NatWest Car Loans

GET A LOAN FAST

&NatWest
The Action Bank

NatWest Car Loans

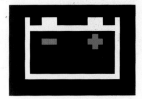

-LESS SNAGS + MORE OPTIONS

&NatWest
The Action Bank

One of the important aspects of Minale Tattersfield's work for National Westminster Bank is that a coordinated image has been maintained despite the sheer diversity of the material produced. Gold Plus is NatWest's premier financial service. The 'precious' theme is delineated with subtlety, while a symbol in the style of an ampersand reflects the complementary nature of benefits to Gold Plus customers.

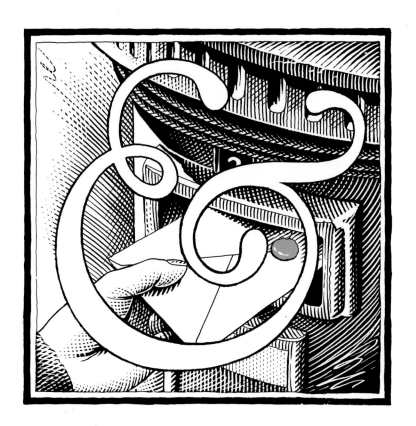

GREECE

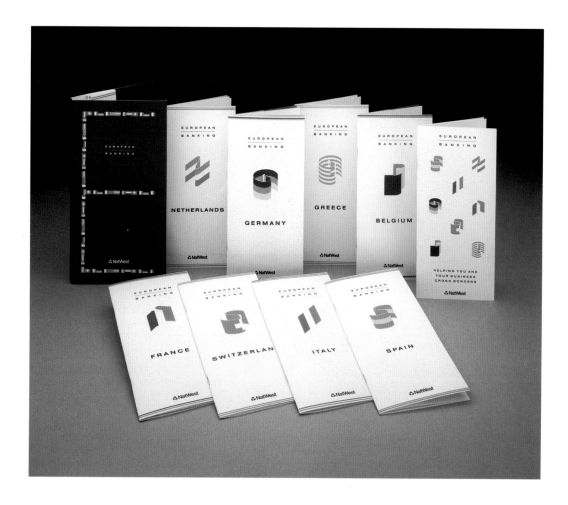

The consultancy has also created a wide variety of specialist material on banking and finance.
This European Banking literature was developed to attract the business customer in anticipation of
the single market of 1992 and will be used by NatWest's European network of over 200 branches.
Each country has its own brochure which is characterised by the national flag shaped in the letter
of that country – for example, G for Greece.

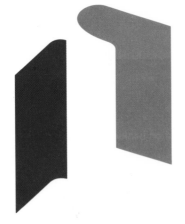

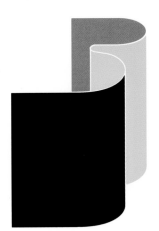

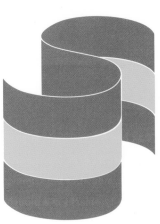

For NatWest's 1988 calendar, the theme of 88 was developed to symbolise the Action Bank's involvement in all aspects of modern life and work. The figure 88 was illustrated in a variety of leisure, industrial and commercial contexts – from the patterns made by oarsmen in water to tractor tyremarks in a ploughed field.

		M	A	R	C	H	
MON	TUE	WED	THUR	FRI	SAT	SUN
	1	2	3	4	5	6
7	8	9	10	11	12	13
14	15	16	17	18	19	20
21	22	23	24	25	26	27
28	29	30	31			

	A	P	R	I	L	
MON	TUE	WED	THUR	FRI	SAT	SUN
				1	2	3
4	5	6	7	8	9	10
11	12	13	14	15	16	17
18	19	20	21	22	23	24
25	26	27	28	29	30	

		M	A	Y		
MON	TUE	WED	THUR	FRI	SAT	SUN
						1
2	3	4	5	6	7	8
9	10	11	12	13	14	15
16	17	18	19	20	21	22
23	24	25	26	27	28	29
30	31					

NatWest
The Action Bank

THE NATWEST TROPHY

Action from the 1988 NatWest Trophy, knock-out cricket tournament is captured by Ian Murray, student of illustration at Kingston Polytechnic in Surrey. The Bank also supports the Ken Barrington Under-13 competition and provides Kwik Cricket equipment for junior players.

A U G U S T

MON	TUE	WED	THUR	FRI	SAT	SUN
	1	2	3	4	5	6
7	8	9	10	11	12	13
14	15	16	17	18	19	20
21	22	23	24	25	26	27
28	29	30	31			

S E P T E M B E R

MON	TUE	WED	THUR	FRI	SAT	SUN
				1	2	3
4	5	6	7	8	9	10
11	12	13	14	15	16	17
18	19	20	21	22	23	24
25	26	27	28	29	30	

O C T O B E R

MON	TUE	WED	THUR	FRI	SAT	SUN
						1
2	3	4	5	6	7	8
9	10	11	12	13	14	15
16	17	18	19	20	21	22
23	24	25	26	27	28	29
30	31					

When National Westminster Bank commissioned a 1989 calendar to reflect its 'action in the community' programme, Minale Tattersfield's solution was to use the resources of British design colleges to create 12 unusual and spectacular images. Students training in different design disciplines were sponsored by the consultancy to produce the work – and further sums were paid to children's charities.

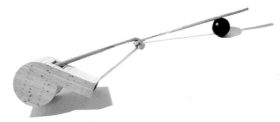

TIME FOR CONSERVATION

The 1990 NatWest calendar was given the
topical theme 'Time for Conservation'.
Illustration and photography were skilfully
combined to enhance the message that
time is running out for the earth's
resources. Among the images, shells,
butterflies and dandelions reflect the
fragile beauty of nature.

SOUTH AMERICAN RAINFORESTS

Although tropical rainforests cover only fourteen
percent of the world's land surface, it is estimated that
they contain half the species on earth. Their
destruction would be the greatest biological disaster
ever perpetrated by man. However, eleven to fifteen
million hectares are being damaged or destroyed
each year. NatWest has provided support, particularly in South America, for WWF's vital work to try to
save the rainforests.

TIME FOR CONSERVATION

MON	TUE	WED	THUR	FRI	SAT	SUN
MARCH						
			1	2	3	4
5	6	7	8	9	10	11
12	13	14	15	16	17	18
19	20	21	22	23	24	25
26	27	28	29	30	31	

APRIL

MON	TUE	WED	THUR	FRI	SAT	SUN
						1
2	3	4	5	6	7	8
9	10	11	12	13	14	15
16	17	18	19	20	21	22
23	24	25	26	27	28	29
30						

MON	TUE	WED	THUR	FRI	SAT	SUN
MAY						
	1	2	3	4	5	6
7	8	9	10	11	12	13
14	15	16	17	18	19	20
21	22	23	24	25	26	27
28	29	30	31			

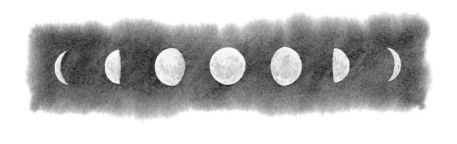

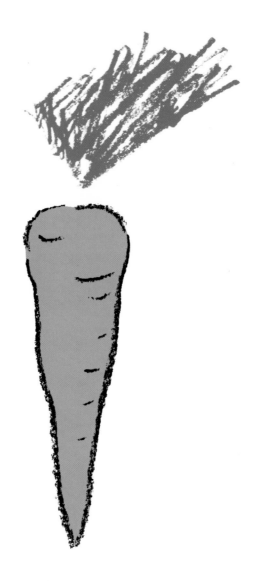

1988 **Thorntons**

1988 **Sammontana**

1990 **Sammontana new range**

1988 **Tesco**

food & **drink**

1985 **Harrods**

1988 **San Pellegrino**

1988 **Irn Bru**

1987 **Hundhaar**

1990 **Beefeater**

1979 **Gilbeys**

1989 **Croft**

1989 **Wine Treasury**

5

'Man, being reasonable,
must get drunk'
(Lord Byron)

Thorntons chocolates are handmade and contain only fresh ingredients. To differentiate the quality of this family confectioner from rivals in its UK and US markets, a new corporate identity was developed using decorative typefaces and scripts to enhance the company's traditional appeal. Assisted by revised packaging, the new identity has seen sales rise by up to 50% in some outlets.

Italian ice cream maker
Sammontana wanted the
packaging for its lollies,
cones and tubs to break
with the garish vulgarity
traditionally associated with
the market. In place of comic
book crudeness, Minale
Tattersfield created a visual
style which was fun but
elegant – and capable of
transition from pack to
van livery.

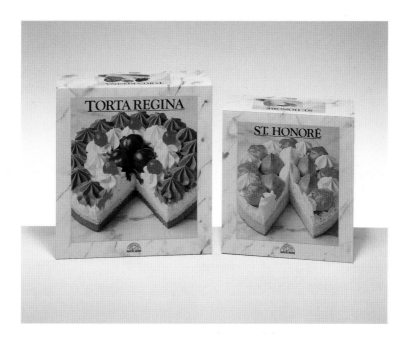

In a country where ice cream is a national institution, there has been
a shift in consumption patterns. Italians no longer confine their ice cream
eating to the summer: pre-packaged ice cream cakes are now enjoyed in
the home all year round. This range was designed for Sammontana, using
a sophisticated marble effect background.

The Cinque Stelle (5 Star) brand is part of the exclusive Gran Gelato range – a veritable constellation of upmarket ice creams and sorbets with exotic ingredients such as candied peach, roasted coffee beans, hazelnuts and fudge.

These tubs are the first stage in a complete update of Sammontana's range. Eventually each product will tell its own individual story: on the opposite page, for instance, Golosa (greedy) speaks for itself.

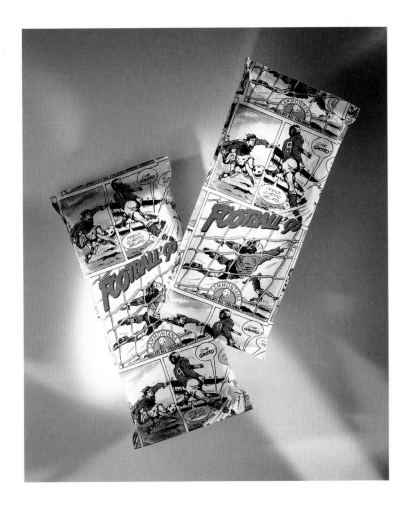

This circular ice lolly is made out of chocolate and vanilla sections in a traditional football pattern. The packaging itself harks back to the halcyon days of the 'Roy of the Rovers' comic strip. Created especially for the 1990 World Cup in Italy, this souvenir should really have the opposition licked.

Tesco's ready meals are a particularly good example of the growing cosmopolitan influence on supermarket food. **Packaging** by Minale Tattersfield for Tesco's Chinese and Continental dishes capture the inherent flavour of each country of origin with wit: the Chinese meals use two lines of type in place of chopsticks while the Continental range uses coloured bars (reflecting the colours of the national flag) on a restaurant menu-style layout.

The Vegetable Selection was the first range completed in this mammoth packaging programme by Minale Tattersfield for Tesco, which involved more than fifty packs. The use of evocative photographs of ingredients indicated the way healthy, vegetarian eating was at last being taken seriously as a sophisticated mainstream trend by the big chains.

TESCO

MEXICAN SELECTION

MICROWAVABLE
SUITABLE FOR HOME FREEZING

CHILLI CON CARNE WITH RICE
MINCED BEEF WITH RED KIDNEY BEANS IN A CHILLI SAUCE SERVED WITH RICE

SERVES ONE

SERVING SUGGESTION

11½ OZ
325 g ℮

BEST BEFORE (2)

PRICE

KEEP REFRIGERATED

TESCO

MEXICAN SELECTION

MICROWAVABLE
SUITABLE FOR HOME FREEZING

CHILLI CON CARNE
MINCED BEEF WITH RED KIDNEY BEANS IN A CHILLI SAUCE

SERVES TWO

SERVING SUGGESTION

1 lb
454 g ℮

BEST BEFORE (2)

PRICE

KEEP REFRIGERATED

The Vegetable Selection was the first range completed in a mammoth packaging programme by Minale Tattersfield for Tesco which involved more than fifty packs. The use of evocative photographs of ingredients indicated the way healthy, vegetarian eating was at last being taken seriously as a sophisticated mainstream trend by the big chains.

VEGETARIANS

TESCO

VEGETABLE SELECTION

GREEN BEANS, CAULIFLOWER, TOMATO & CARROTS IN A CREAMY CHEESE SAUCE TOPPED WITH GRATED POTATO

MICROWAVABLE
SUITABLE FOR HOME FREEZING

FRESH VEGETABLE BAKE
SERVE AS A MAIN MEAL FOR ONE OR AS AN ACCOMPANYING VEGETABLE FOR MORE

15 oz 425 g ℮	BEST BEFORE (2)	PRICE
KEEP REFRIGERATED		

TESCO

VEGETABLE SELECTION

SUITABLE FOR HOME FREEZING

POTATO SLICES WITH A CHEESE & ONION SAUCE

CHEESY POTATO BAKE
SERVE AS A MAIN MEAL FOR ONE OR AS AN ACCOMPANYING VEGETABLE FOR MORE

454 g 1 lb ℮	BEST BEFORE (2)	PRICE
KEEP REFRIGERATED		

While it would be wrong to throw oil on Harrods' troubled waters… this packaging exemplifies the fine work Minale Tattersfield has done for the store over the years. The Neo-Impressionist illustration style was created by Brian Tattersfield.

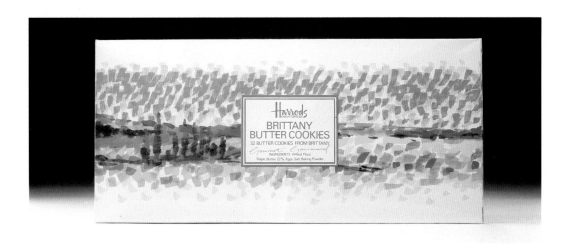

When San Pellegrino of Italy introduced a range of four fruit juices which consisted of 100 per cent juice and no additives, the content was communicated using two relevant fruits to make up the all-important percentage. 100 per cent for ingenuity in thinking up the idea.

Irn Bru, made by A. G. Barr, is Scotland's favourite soft drink. It has cult status and, in particular, 'street credibility' among children (unlike Coke, which is viewed as a product of global marketing). **Minale Tattersfield** was asked to give the brand its first update since 1949 in view of plans to market it more widely in other regions of the UK and in mainland Europe. The graphic imagery was simplified and strengthened. The engraving of a Victorian weightlifter on the original bottle was transformed into an asexual athlete who proved more appealing to modern consumers. **Since** the redesign, sales of Irn Bru have been growing at a rate of 76 per cent a year.

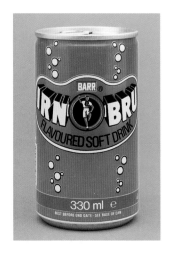

Minale Tattersfield often presents new ideas to Italian drinks giant,
San Pellegrino. Some, alas – like Cab – don't see the light but Spell,
Britonic (traditional G & T sailing imagery), and One-O-One
(a successful Coke competitor) sell well.

Hundhaar means, literally, 'hair of the dog'. Appropriately Germanic branding for a new Schnapps product enabled Irish Distillers to target the affluent young, the thinking behind the product – supported by Minale Tattersfield's packaging – being that Schnapps could become the next cult in the drinks market: a chaser to the Continental lager boom.

Careful redesigns have enabled Beefeater and Gilbey's London Dry Gin, two classic British brands, to recapture their traditional appeal. Familiar graphic elements of the past have been combined with new colours and typography to suggest more sophisticated products.

Croft is an International Distillers and Vintners brand associated almost exclusively with sherry. But Croft has also been shipping port to the UK for 300 years. Minale Tattersfield was therefore commissioned to redesign Croft's five leading port brands in order to raise their market profile. Each bottle has a traditional seal with a stylised vertical brushmark, the colours of these brushmarks denoting the quality of the port.

MIJANOU BLECH

The Wine Treasury Ltd.

143 EBURY STREET
LONDON SW1W 9QN
TELEPHONE 01-730 6774 AND
01-730 4099 FAX 01-823 6402

When Belgravia restaurateurs Neville and Sonia Blech set up The Wine Treasury as a new venture, Minale Tattersfield's identity for the company appropriately explored traditional vinicultural symbols in sepia colours. **But** there's a twist: the keys to the wine vault are also the keys to the wine itself. Definitely a solution which improves with age…

The Wine Treasury Ltd.

143 EBURY STREET, LONDON SW1W 9QN
TELEPHONE 01-730 6774 AND 01-730 4099

1988 **SR toothpaste**

1984 **Boots pet food**

1987 **Thorntons**

shopping & **fashion**

1982 **Heal's**

1989 **Oy Stockmann**

1988 **Coin**

1989 **Napoleonerba**

1989 **Mantero**

1986 **Giorgio Armani**

1986 **Ragno**

1989 **Oliview**

6

'A man without a smiling
face must not open a shop'
(Chinese proverb)

Health, vitality and freshness were the key themes for the repackaging of Gibbs SR toothpaste – a well-established brand over 50 years old and in need of a brush-up.

One of the great missed marketing opportunities of the '80s? Boots wanted to personalise its canned pet foods without showing specific breeds and without costly reproduction of illustration or photography. By using the famous Boots logo as the animal's nose and adding simple graphic elements to distinguish dogs from cats, a unique brand identity was achieved. The client didn't see the ingenious use of its corporate logo in quite the same spirit, so the scheme was filed under 'Ones That Got Away'.

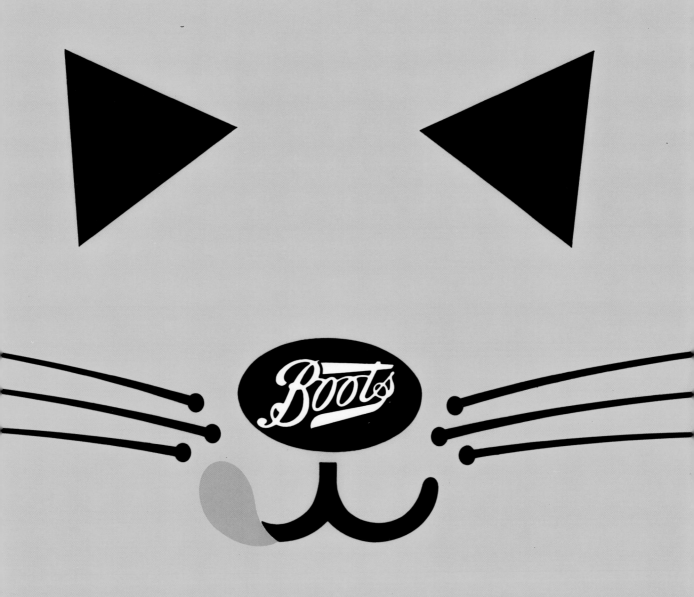

Family confectioners since 1911, Thorntons wanted a new corporate identity to apply to all aspects of its rapidly expanding business without losing its traditional appeal. An emphasis on decorative scripts and fresh colours in developing the elements of the identity resulted in an image which has significantly boosted sales in Thornton's chocolate shops.

This must be one of the shortest-lived corporate identities of all time – but its lasting influence on high street trends bears no relation to its own abrupt disappearance. Within a year of Minale Tattersfield devising a classic new image for Heal's – one which evoked the commercial coming-of-age of the Arts and Crafts Movement by taking a chequered pattern used by Sir Ambrose Heal as his trademark – the store was bought by another design knight, Sir Terence Conran. Out went the identity but observers still remember with affection its supreme versatility, from van liveries and store fronts to Christmas promotions.

The best of French design and culture throughout April at

HEALS

196 Tottenham Court Road, London W1A 1BJ. Telephone: 01-636 1666
and Tunsgate, Guildford. Telephone: 767156

Finland's premier department store Stockmanns has been described as
'the Harrods of Helsinki'. Minale Tattersfield headed a consortium of
British designers – including Maurice Broughton Associates and
Pennington Robson – in a spectacular refurbishment of the 1930s store.
The work required a special attention to detail given the architectural
pedigree of the building, which was originally designed by Sigurd
Frosterus. **The** store also has a new extension by Kristian Gullichsen,
whose mother worked with the legendary Alvar Aalto. This has
increased retail space from 120,000 sq ft to 200,000 sq ft, so necessi-
tating the refurbishment. The Minale Tattersfield masterplan created
a calm, classic environment with a 'discovery' around every corner.

Commissioned to create a series of identities for the different divisions of leading Italian fashion retailer Coin Spa, Minale Tattersfield devised brandnames adaptable enough to work in a variety of display, packaging and labelling contexts. Coexis, based on engraved Roman characters, is aimed at 25-35 year old women desiring elegance and sophistication. Jottun is for men of the same age group, seeking a masculine but stylish image. The bold, simple Green Village targets children, with two arrows denoting growth. Exiozi – the name stems from the Irish colloquial term for the children's game of noughts and crosses – is the teenage division.

GREEN

VILLAGE

exi·ozi

Fashion company Napoleonerba sells exclusive knitwear and polo shirts through its many Italian outlets. Minale Tattersfield's updated image addressed the problem of incorporating a symbol on the polo shirts by taking the N and E of the company name to be embroidered as an emblem. Counter displays were also created to support the new image: a wintry Scottish castle scene reflects the Shetland jumper range, while sea and sun promote the short-sleeved polo shirt.

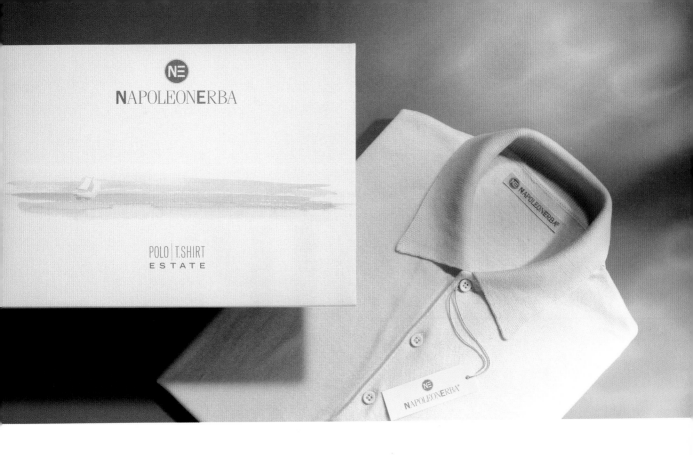

VIII

MANTERO _VIII

Pieces of eight: the Mantero group, supplier of silk to leading couturiers throughout the world since 1820, is today run by eight brothers and has eight operating companies. Minale Tattersfield's identity, devised to link the entire group, is based on the Roman numeral for eight: this manifests itself in a stylish symbol denoting the M of Mantero. The group's clients include Armani, Chanel and Yves St. Laurent.

Few names sum up Italian high fashion, design and style better than Giorgio Armani. A commission from the company to design packaging for a new range of swimwear and underwear gave Minale Tattersfield the opportunity to bring its own creative credentials to bear. **The** resulting packs are highly imaginative and practical: each box has understated graphics and is in two parts, sliding together to form the letter A. **The** swimwear packaging in particular subscribes to the idea that the best ideas are often the simplest: it is water-resistant, pocket-sized and made of high impact polystyrene.

ragno®

It is said the Italians are stylish right down to their underwear. Now we know the truth. Minale Tattersfield's design work for old-established Italian underwear manufacturer Ragno brought the company into line with the latest fashion trends by creating a new image and rationalising its packaging.

Browns

Browns (South Molton Street) Limited, 23-27 South Molton Street, London W1Y 1DA
Telephone: 01-491 7833

OLIVIEW®

Created to promote the young fashion line of Valentino Rome, this logotype centres the V of Valentino in a custom identity.